OSCAR WILDE

The Importance of Being Earnest
Bieng Earnest

A Trivial Play for Serious People

With a Commentary and Chronology by
PATRICIA HERN

and Notes by
GLENDA LEEMING

D0063445

Methuen Student Editions
METHUEN · LONDON

A METHUEN PAPERBACK

This Methuen Student Edition first published in 1981 by
Eyre Methuen Ltd., 11 New Fetter Lane, London EC4P 4EE.
Reprinted 1983 (twice) and 1986 by Methuen London Ltd.
Commentary, Chronology and Notes © 1981 by Eyre Methuen Ltd.
Printed in Great Britain by Richard Clay (The Chaucer Press), Ltd.,
Bungay, Suffolk

ISBN 0 413 396 30 4

*Thanks are due to James Gibbs, Malcolm Page and Non Worrall for their
help and advice in the preparation of this edition.*

Contents

Six pages of illustrations appear at the end of the Commentary after page xxxvi.

Oscar Wilde: 1854 - 1900

> I was a man who stood in symbolic relation to the art and
> culture of my age. [. . .] I made art a philosophy, and
> philosophy an art: I altered the minds of men and the colours
> of things: there was nothing I said or did that did not make
> people wonder: I took the drama, the most objective form
> known to art, and made it as personal a mode of expression as
> the lyric or the sonnet, at the same time that I widened its
> range and enriched its characterisation. [. . .] I awoke the
> imagination of my century so that it created myth and legend
> around me: I summed up all systems in a phrase, and all
> existence in an epigram. (Rupert Hart-Davis, *Selected Letters
> of Oscar Wilde*, p.194)

Oscar Wilde made that uncompromising claim to greatness in
unlikely circumstances: he was serving a two-year prison sentence
in Reading Gaol, convicted of gross indecency, a declared bankrupt,
a man considered unfit to have custody of or even contact with his
children, pilloried in the national press, condemned by respectable
Victorian society. For many, Wilde's life illustrated the dangerous
affinity between the principles of aesthetics and unprincipled
practices of decadence. Oscar Wilde's statement here is taken from
a long letter known as *De Profundis*, written to Lord Alfred
Douglas (1870-1945), the third son of the Marquess of Queensberry
(1844-1900), whose intimacy with Wilde led to the sensational
trials and the disgrace which ended Wilde's brilliant career as a wit,
bon viveur, poet, dramatist and aesthete in fashionable London
society. The highly publicised scandal has coloured much critical
assessment of Wilde as a writer. He himself asserted that his
life and his art were inextricably woven together as a testament to
Beauty, being deliberately organised and ornamented with more
regard for Beauty than for what Victorian society understood as
morality. He delighted in remarks such as: 'I treated Art as the
supreme reality and life as a mere mode of fiction.' (*De Profundis*,
in *Selected Letters*, p.194) The French writer, André Gide (1871-
1951), recalled Oscar Wilde delivering a similar epigram during a

conversation in 1895: 'Would you like to know the great drama of my life? It's that I've put my genius into my life; I've put only my talent into my work.'

1854   Born in Dublin on 16 October, a younger son of a successful surgeon, Sir William Wilde, and his wife, a well known Irish writer.

1864
  -71   A boarder at Portora Royal School.

1871
  -74   Read Classics at Trinity College, Dublin.

1874   February: won the Berkeley Gold Medal for Greek.

1874   A Demyship (Classics scholarship) at Magdalen College,
  -78   Oxford.

1876   Travelled in Italy.

1877   Visited Ravenna and Greece.

1878   Newdigate Prize for his poem *Ravenna*.

1878   Graduated from Oxford with First Class Honours. Took a house in London and became an accepted part of that section of London society which interested itself in the theatre, music, painting and witty conversation.

1881   *Poems* published. They won some critical approval but little serious interest. 'The author possesses cleverness, astonishing fluency, a rich and full vocabulary, and nothing to say.' (*The Saturday Review*, 23 July 1881)

1882   Lecture tour of United States of America, arranged by Richard D'Oyly Carte (1844-1901), a theatrical impresario who had founded a company for the production of comic operas with libretti by Sir W.S. Gilbert (1836-1911) and music by Sir Arthur Sullivan (1842-1900). Since it was popularly held that Wilde had provided the model for the ludicrous character of Bunthorne, a 'fleshly poet' in Gilbert and Sullivan's opera *Patience* (1881) which D'Oyly Carte was taking to America, D'Oyly Carte saw Wilde's presence as an unusual and probably effective means of publicising the production, while at the same time providing a key to some of the opera's jokes.

1882   Wrote his first play, *Vera*. Completed *The Duchess of Padua* (a tragedy in the Jacobean mould) in Paris.

1884   Married Constance Lloyd.

1885   Settled in London at 16, Tite Street, Chelsea, a house flamboyantly adapted and decorated by the artist and architect E.W. Godwin.

June: his first son, Cyril, born.

1886 November: his second son, Vyvyan, born.

1887 Edited the journal *Woman's World* with the ambition that
-88 it should become 'the recognised organ for the expression
of women's opinions on all subjects of literature, art, and
modern life, and yet it should be a magazine that men could
read with pleasure, and consider it a privilege to contribute
to'. (*Selected Letters*, p.68)

1888 *The Happy Prince and Other Tales* published; praised for
their 'charming fancies and quaint humour'. (*Athenaeum*,
September 1888)

1889 Published an essay, *The Portrait of Mr.W.H.*, claiming to
prove that Shakespeare had written his sonnets for a boy
actor called William Hughes rather than for the Earl of
Southampton.

1890 *The Picture of Dorian Gray* published. This, his only novel,
created a considerable stir: many critics were shocked by
the story of a beautiful young man whose portrait, hidden
from public view, reflects the ravages of his life of crime and
debauchery while he himself remains magically unchanged
in appearance until the moment of his death. The *Daily
Chronicle* of 30 June 1890 called it 'a poisonous book'.

1891 *Lord Arthur Savile's Crime and Other Stories* published,
also *Intentions* in which he discussed his ideas on the nature
of Art and the responsibility of the Artist. *A House of
Pomegranates*, a second group of fairy stories, was published
the same year. Began work on *Salomé* in Paris, writing in
French. Met Lord Alfred Douglas, then a young and good-
looking Oxford undergraduate attracted by Wilde's
sophistication and success.

1892 *Lady Windermere's Fan* presented at the St James's Theatre,
London, by the actor-manager Sir George Alexander (1858-
1918). It was a popular success but won only rather
grudging praise from the reviewers. 'For the staleness of the
incidents one has only to refer to half a dozen familiar
French plays.' (Arthur Walkley, a respected contemporary
critic writing in the *Speaker*.) 'All the men talk like
Mr Oscar Wilde. Everything is discussed paradoxically.'
(*The Speaker*, 27 February 1892) 'The dialogue is
exquisitely funny, is satirical without being aggravating to
the audience. It is biting, and at the same time genial and

good-humoured.' (*Westminster Review*) This last review, however, also dismissed the plot as 'very improbable — impossible, one might almost add'.

1892 Began work on *A Woman of No Importance* for actor-manager Sir Herbert Beerbohm Tree (1853-1917).

1893 February: *Salomé* published in France, but also distributed in England. *A Woman of No Importance* produced by Herbert Tree at the Theatre Royal, Haymarket, in London. Critical comment was again dismissive of the plot but appreciative of the wit.

> The story, an extremely slight one for four acts, cannot be regarded as pleasant or satisfactory. [. . .] The dialogue is brilliant, epigrammatic, paradoxical, antithetical even to a fault. (*The Saturday Review*)

1894 Lord Alfred Douglas's English translation of *Salomé* was published, with illustrations by Aubrey Beardsley (1872-98). Performance of this play was impossible in England at that time since the Lord Chamberlain's Office (responsible for theatre censorship) had ruled that it was unacceptable to represent Biblical events on the stage. It was produced in Paris by Sarah Bernhardt (1845-1923), the leading actress of her day. *The Sphinx* published.

1895 January: *An Ideal Husband* opened at the Theatre Royal, Haymarket. The novelist H.G. Wells (1886-1946) reviewed it in the *Pall Mall Gazette*:

> In many ways his new production is diverting, and even where the fun is not of the rarest character the play remains interesting. And, among other things, it marks an interesting phase in the dramatic development of the author. [. . .] Oscar Wilde is, so to speak, working his way to innocence, as others work towards experience — is sloughing his epigrams slowly but surely, and discovering to an appreciative world, beneath the attenuated veil of his wit, that he, too, has a heart.

February: *The Importance of Being Earnest* was produced with great success by George Alexander at the St James's Theatre, London. It won praise from reviewers, such as the critic of the London *Times*, Hamilton Fyfe, writing on this occasion for the *New York Times*:

Oscar Wilde may be said to have at last, and by a single
stroke, put his enemies under his feet. [. . .] The thing
is slight in structure and as devoid of purpose as a paper
balloon, but it is extraordinarily funny, and the universal
assumption is that it will remain on the boards here for
an indefinitely extended period.

One enemy whom Wilde conspicuously failed to put 'under
his feet' was the Marquess of Queensberry, the father of
Lord Alfred Douglas, who accused Wilde of alienating
Douglas from his family and corrupting him. His explicit
charge of gross indecency drove Wilde to sue him for
criminal libel, against the advice of his friends, who feared
the effect on Wilde's life and career of such a public
scandal, even if he won his case. After a series of damaging
testimonies against him, Wilde was compelled to withdraw
his suit, then was himself arrested.
May: after two trials Wilde was found guilty of immoral and
indecent conduct and sentenced to two years' imprisonment
with hard labour.
November: he was transferred from Wandsworth Prison in
London to Reading Gaol,where he served the rest of his
sentence. It is important to understand that homosexuality
was not only illegal in England at this time, but considered
unspeakably decadent and corrupting by conventional
Victorian society, although known to exist in bohemian or
artistic circles as well as in military and naval life – there it
was tolerated because remote from the centres of public
activity and social behaviour. Wilde was not discreet or
decorous enough to escape notoriety; he forced society to
take an attitude to his relationship with Douglas, and society
was outraged.

1897   In Reading Gaol he wrote a long letter to Douglas, later
published under the title *De Profundis*.

1895   Wilde found the ugliness, brutality and degradation of
-97   prison life hard to endure. At first the isolation, the meagre
food, the squalor and the boredom made him fear for his
sanity. His suffering was aggravated by the bankruptcy
proceedings against him, by his mother's death, his wife's
action to establish a legal separation, and the court order
forbidding him any further contact with his two sons.

I have lain in prison for nearly two years. Out of my

> nature has come wild despair; an abandonment to grief
> that was piteous to look at; terrible and impotent rage:
> bitterness and scorn: anguish that wept aloud: misery
> that could find no voice: sorrow that was dumb.
> (*Selected Letters*, p.195)

However, before his release he appeared to have come to
terms with his situation, seeing it as a means of growing
spiritually and intellectually.

1897   May: released from prison, travelled to France, then to
Italy with Douglas. Began to work on the poem *The Ballad
of Reading Gaol* in which he tried to convey the degree of
brutilisation and isolation endured in prison, giving the
poem dramatic focus through the story of a prisoner
sentenced to death for the murder of his mistress, whose
execution disturbs the whole life of the prison and demands
some distinct moral or philosophical response from the
poet-observer. He also wrote to the newspapers on the
subject of prison reform.

1898   *The Ballad of Reading Gaol* was published, meeting with a
mixed response from the critics: some were moved by what
they felt to be its passionate authenticity; others saw it as a
spurious bid for sympathy. At least one reviewer, however,
wrote of the poem in a way which Wilde himself
acknowledged to be just and perceptive:

> We see a great spectacular intellect, to which, at last,
> pity and terror have come in their own person, and no
> longer as puppets in a play. [. . .] This poem, then, is
> partly a plea on behalf of prison reform: and, so far as
> it is written with that aim, it is not art. [. . .] For the
> poem is not really a ballad at all, but a sombre, angry,
> interrupted reverie; and it is the subcurrent of
> meditation, it is the asides, which count, not the story,
> as a story, of the drunken soldier who was hanged for
> killing a woman. (*The Saturday Review*, March 1898)

1898   December: Wilde returned to Paris.
1900   30 November: died of meningitis in Paris.
1905   *De Profundis* published.

The obituaries which appeared in the British Press reflected the
ambivalent attitude towards Wilde which has, to some extent,

survived to this day. The *Pall Mall Gazette* declared:

> Mr Wilde had wonderful cleverness, but no substantiality. His
> plays were full of bright moments, but devoid of consideration
> as drama. [. . .] He was content, for the most part, that his
> characters should sit about and talk paradoxes. [. . .] His most
> useful influence was as a corrective to British stolidity, but it
> was too diffuse to be worth much even at that.

Max Beerbohm, dramatic critic of the *Saturday Review* from 1898
to 1910, rated Wilde more highly:

> He was not a mere maker of plays. [. . .] He came as a thinker,
> a weaver of ideas, and as a wit, and as the master of literary
> style.

Some years later the critic, W.M. Leadman, writing in the
Westminster Review of August 1906, tried to see the relationship
between Wilde's life and his art in a more objective although
basically sympathetic way:

> His whole literary work (plays, poems, essays and fiction) in
> vain cried out for just criticism — prejudice, misconception, and
> a strained sense of respectability refused it. [. . .] Wilde was
> always considered a mere 'poseur'. [. . .] Great and undue stress
> was invariably laid on the man's eccentricities; in the public eye
> Wilde was only a witty fellow yearning for celebrity and capable
> of performing weird literary antics to obtain that object. He is
> indeed a tragic figure. [. . .] And yet, leaving the question of his
> conduct on one side, his sole fault was simply his unswerving
> fidelity to his own intellectual bias. He could not write about
> ordinary things in an ordinary way. [. . .] He was incapable of
> moulding his maxims on the traditional conceptions of virtue
> and vice.

Commentary

Wilde's aesthetics: the science of the beautiful

> A work of art is useless as a flower is useless. A flower blossoms for its own joy. We gain a moment of joy by looking at it. (*Selected Letters*, p.96)

> The pleasure one has in creating a work of art is a purely personal pleasure, and it is for the sake of this pleasure that one creates. (To the Editor of the *Scots Observer*, July 1890: *Selected Letters*, p.81)

> Whatever I touched I made beautiful in a new mode of beauty. (*Selected Letters*, p.194)

These statements express an attitude to art which is the basis of Wilde's 'science of the beautiful' — the phrase he used to define aesthetics for the benefit of an American journalist in 1882.

While at Oxford, between 1874 and 1878, Wilde was looking for some creed or set of principles which could give shape and expression to his own passionate appreciation of objects, experiences or ideas whose symmetry of form, or harmony and brilliance of decoration apparently separated them from common-place realities. The prosaic Victorian world of rapid industrialisation, its cities begrimed with soot and polluted by slums, was one such reality. Another was the kind of morality which seemed to mistrust pleasure, glorifying instead unsmiling toil for material gain as some guarantee of virtue, and imprisoning the imagination while encouraging hypocrisy and intolerance. This world had already been pictured and condemned by writers like Charles Dickens (1812-70) in, for example, his novels *Hard Times* (1855) and *Little Dorrit* (1857). Wilde was attracted by the English revival of Catholicism among some academics, known as the Oxford Movement and led by men such as Cardinal Newman (1801-90). In this Anglo-Catholicism (separate from Roman Catholicism) there was a renewed delight in ritual and mysticism not found in the Protestant traditions.

In March 1887 Wilde wrote to a friend:

> I have a dream of a visit to Newman, of the holy sacrament in a
> new Church, and of a quiet and peace afterwards in my soul. I
> need not say, though, that I shift with every breath of thought
> and am weaker and more self-deceiving than ever.
>   If I could hope that the Church would wake in me some
> earnestness and purity I would go over *as a luxury,* if for no
> better reason. But I can hardly hope it would, and to go over to
> Rome would be to sacrifice and give up my two great gods,
> 'Money and Ambition'. (*Selected Letters,* p.12)

He did not formally join the Roman Catholic Church until he was
dying in Paris in 1900. Instead, as a young man he found that his
belief in the importance of Beauty as a guiding principle could be
married to his enjoyment of material comforts and social success
in the service of Art. Wilde was not an innovator; his older
contemporaries, John Ruskin (1819-1900), Slade Professor of Fine
Art and author of many essays and articles on painting and
architecture, and Walter Pater (1839-94), a Fellow of Brasenose
College, Oxford, who had established himself as an authority on
Aesthetics with the publication of *Studies in the History of the
Renaissance* in 1873, had both already preached the doctrine of
'Art for Art's sake', representing the search for Beauty as a noble
vocation, a new morality. A group of painters known as the
Pre-Raphaelites were adapting the ideas of Ruskin and Pater in
their exploration of a style freed from the restrictions of naturalistic
perspective and familiar subjects. They drew images from Celtic as
well as Classical mythology and presented them with a richness of
detailed decoration which owed much to medieval church paintings
and illuminated manuscripts. Shortly after leaving Oxford, Wilde
spent time in Paris and London with some leaders of the Pre-
Raphaelite movement, including the painter Millais (1829-96) and
the painter and poet Dante Gabriel Rossetti (1828-82).

    When, in May 1891, Wilde published *Intentions,* a collection of
dialogues explaining his artistic principles, he emphasised the
importance of Art for Art's sake rather than as a vehicle for
religious or social instruction. He presented Beauty and wit rather
than naturalism or work-a-day morality as the Artist's proper
concerns. He now developed the idea which he had put forward
in July 1890 when defending *The Picture of Dorian Gray* against
accusations of decadence and obscenity; then he had written, 'An
artist, sir, has no ethical sympathies at all. Virtue and weakness

are to him simply what the colours on his palette are to the painter'. (*Selected Letters*, p.81) Even later, in prison, paying a heavy price for putting his principles into practice, Wilde insisted upon the Artist's necessary freedom to seek experiences beyond the boundaries permitted by society:

> People thought it dreadful of me to have entertained at dinner the evil things of life, and to have found pleasure in their company. But they, from the point of view through which I, as an artist in life, approached them, were delightfully suggestive and stimulating. It was like feasting with panthers. (*Selected Letters*, p.220)

Using a witty mouthpiece for his own views in the dialogue 'The Decay of Lying', Wilde rejected the Romantic reverence for Nature and the Victorians' preoccupation with the practical details of their daily routines. Nature, he asserted, was lamentably crude and unshaped, far from being the source of moral enlightenment or poetic sensibility as, for example, the poet Wordsworth (1770-1850) had claimed it to be in his Preface to the *Lyrical Ballads* and in poems such as 'Lines Written Above Tintern Abbey' or 'The Prelude'. Wilde's spokesman, Vivian, declares:

> What Art really reveals to us is Nature's lack of design, her curious crudities, her extraordinary monotony, her absolutely unfinished condition. [. . .] Art is our spirited protest, our gallant attempt to teach Nature her proper place. ('The Decay of Lying', in *Intentions*, 1891)

Vivian goes on to argue that Art takes life as its raw material to be reshaped into something entirely new, 'and keeps between herself and reality the impenetrable barrier of beautiful style, of decorative or ideal treatment'. This removal from daily life, the sense of being an artefact and therefore somehow artificial in a disturbing way, was noted and regretted by some critics who were otherwise sympathetic to Wilde's work. Even Wilde seems to have been aware of the dangers inherent in his attitude; in a letter to the writer of the Sherlock Holmes stories, Arthur Conan Doyle (1859-1930), he observed:

> Between me and life there is a mist of words always. I throw probability out of the window for the sake of a phrase, and the chance of an epigram makes me desert truth. Still, I do aim at making a work of art. (*Selected Letters*, p.95)

He displayed contempt for 'the people', seeing the Artist as
isolated from the crowd by his genius and then persecuted for his
strangeness by those classes of society categorised by the essayist
and poet Matthew Arnold (1822-88) as Barbarians (the aristocracy)
and Philistines (the affluent middle class). As for the working class,
in one of the dialogues, 'The Critic as Artist', Wilde wrote
despairingly:

> We live in the age of the overworked, and the undereducated;
> the age in which people are so industrious that they become
> absolutely stupid. [. . .] Those who try to lead the people can
> only do so by following the mob.

Later in the same dialogue the leading character remarks: 'Yes, the
public is wonderfully tolerant. It forgives everything except genius.'
These sentiments make Wilde's choice of the theatre as a vehicle
for *his* genius seem like an act of defiance. Certainly his cynicism
about Victorian England is reflected in his portrayal of a society
peopled largely by dilettantes, charlatans and privileged fools. Even
his heroes, like Lord Goring in *An Ideal Husband,* affect an air of
frivolous conceit to hide their true worth. In *The Importance of
Being Earnest* Lady Bracknell says: 'Never speak disrespectfully of
Society, Algernon. Only people who can't get into it do that'. (p.63)
Wilde's attitude was ambivalent: on the one hand, he enjoyed his
personal success in the fashionable world of London's salons,
restaurants and theatres, using the wealth and the way of life he
found there both to inspire and to set off his own wit; on the other
hand, he was evidently aware of its complacency, its artificiality, its
hypocrisy, its cruelty towards those it felt threatened by or could
not place comfortably. He drew on his knowledge of Society and,
to a large extent, depended on his audience's recognition of the
manners and the social taboos governing the characters' actions.
This direct reference to the real world in his own plays may seem
inconsistent in one who condemned contemporary English
melodrama because: 'The characters in these plays talk on the
stage exactly as they would talk off it; they have neither aspirations
nor aspirates; they are taken directly from life and reproduce its
vulgarity down to the smallest detail.' ('The Decay of Lying', in
Intentions, 1891) However, Wilde's plays do not simply hold up a
mirror to nature, rather they present an elaborate and stylised
vision, or revision, of carefully selected images. A contemporary
critic and dramatist, St.John Hankin, remarked that Wilde
presented only 'brilliant surface', never the soul of the character.

This was a deliberate decision by Wilde, not an artistic failure; in
'The Decay of Lying' the protagonist, Vivian, sees the nineteenth
century's struggle to reveal human nature in Art as leading only to
boring uniformity, since what distinguishes one man from his
neighbour are external features such as dress, manners, appearance
and voiced opinions — man discovered through his behaviour in
company, not through solitary soul-searchings or communion with
Nature. At the end of the dialogue Vivian sums up the guiding
principles of 'the new aesthetics':

> Briefly, then, they are these. Art never expresses anything but
> itself. It has an independent life. [. . .] It is not necessarily
> realistic in an age of realism, nor spiritual in an age of faith. [. . .]
>
> The second doctrine is this. All bad art comes from returning
> to Life and Nature, and elevating them into ideals. [. . .] As a
> method Realism is a complete failure. [. . .]
>
> The third doctrine is that Life imitates Art far more than Art
> imitates Life. This results not merely from Life's imitative
> instinct, but from the fact that the self-conscious aim of Life is
> to find expression, and that Art offers it certain beautiful forms
> through which it may realise that energy. [. . .]
>
> The final revelation is that Lying, the telling of beautiful
> untrue things, is the proper aim of Art. (*Intentions* 1891)

Wilde's comic conventions

Wilde's concern with 'brilliant surface' placed him within a
recognisable English tradition. In presenting Society to Society, with
its heroes as those who were most accomplished, most elegant and
most successful in the 'beau monde', and mocking interlopers from
the vulgar world of commerce or the colonies, Wilde revived the
spirit of the late seventeenth-century Restoration Comedy, the
style of Congreve (1670-1729) and Wycherley (1640-1716).
Congreve's comic scenes, for instance, depend upon the audience's
acceptance of an etiquette governing all aspects of social life, so
that a gaffe was recognisable and laughable. The wit was polished,
sophisticated and elitist. It worked through highly structured
word-play rather than slapstick or clowning. In *The Way of the
World* (1700), Congreve's lovers advance their relationship
through a series of verbal duels.

> MILLAMANT. One no more owes one's beauty to a lover than
>   one's wit to an echo: they can but reflect what we look and say;
>   vain, empty things if we are silent or unseen and want a being.

> MIRABELL. Yet, to those two vain, empty things, you owe two
> of the greatest pleasures of your life.
> MILLAMANT. How so?
> MIRABELL. To your lover you owe the pleasure of hearing
> yourselves praised; and to an echo the pleasure of hearing
> yourselves talk.

Poise rather than passion is, similarly, the feature of Wilde's scenes
of courtship.

Just as the small theatres of the Restoration period catered for
an exclusive, privileged and leisured class, so the audiences at the
St. James's Theatre or the Theatre Royal, Haymarket, in the 1890's
were predominantly either rich and aristocratic or fashionably
bohemian. The 1860's and 1870's had seen a change in London's
theatrical life: crude farces, bawdy burlesques and sensational
melodramas no longer dominated the stages of the fashionable West
End. Under the influence of actor-managers like Sir Herbert Tree,
George Alexander and Sir Henry Irving (1838-1905) and of playwrights such as Tom Robertson (1829-71), Society no longer had
to rely upon the Opera for acceptable — or respectable —
entertainment. With a series of plays, including *Society* (1865)
and *Caste* (1867), produced at the Prince of Wales's Theatre in
London, Robertson inaugurated what has been called 'the cup-and-
saucer drama' since it dealt with realistic, contemporary domestic
life. Wilde referred scornfully to the characters: 'they present the
gait, manner, costume and accent of real people; they would pass
unnoticed in a third-class railway carriage'. ('The Decay of Lying')
Yet he benefited from the creation of a new and influential
audience. By February 1895, when *The Importance of Being
Earnest* opened at the St. James's Theatre, Florence Alexander
(wife of the theatre's actor-manager) could write:

> Our first nights at the St. James's Theatre were like brilliant
> parties. Everybody knew everybody, everybody put on their
> best clothes, everybody wished us success. (Cited by A. E. W.
> Mason in *Sir George Alexander at the St. James's Theatre.*)

Wilde's characters are defined by their social status and revealed
through their manners in a way, therefore, that perfectly
complemented the interests and experience of his patrons. They
belong to recognisable groups: the witty young man-about-town
in search of amusement and a rich wife; the daunting dowager or
formidable mother of such an eligible heiress; the glamorous and

often dangerous woman-of-the-world, full of biting wit and sophistication but — because of the worldliness and wickedness which made her attractive — only to be flirted with and not welcomed into the family; the ingenue, a sweet young girl, precocious in manner perhaps but still uncorrupted by experience of the world and delightfully rich. These required the presence of a servant class equally governed by etiquette and nice distinctions of rank; for example, the imperturbable Lane in *The Importance of Being Earnest*.

The Importance of Being Earnest: plot summary

Initially the play was written in four acts; however, while it was in rehearsal Wilde accepted the advice of the actor-manager, George Alexander, and reduced it to three acts, now the accepted version.

Act I

In his luxurious apartment in a fashionable part of London, Algernon Moncrieff awaits the arrival for tea of his aunt, Lady Bracknell. He is surprised by the intrusion of his wealthy and slightly less frivolous friend, up from the country, especially to propose to Lady Bracknell's daughter, Gwendolen. Algernon's curiosity has been roused by the inscription inside this friend's cigarette case which had been left behind on a previous visit. He discovers that the man he calls Ernest Worthing is really named John (or Jack) Worthing. This is the name he answers to when on his country estate performing his duties as guardian of the young heiress, Cecily Cardew. Jack explains that he has had to invent a younger brother called Ernest in order to justify his frequent visits to London to escape from the moral responsibilities involved in his role as guardian. Algy hails this as a variation on his own habit of 'Bunburying'. (Bunbury is an imaginary invalid whose health requires Algy's presence in the country whenever he needs an excuse to leave London.) Jack is alarmed by Algy's lively interest in the idea of Cecily. Algy offers to keep Lady Bracknell occupied while Jack — or 'Ernest' — proposes to Gwendolen, so, shortly after the ladies are ushered in, Algy takes Lady Bracknell off to the music room, leaving Jack to declare his intentions, haltingly, to Gwendolen. She takes the initiative, declaring that she has always loved him for his name, Ernest, and refusing to consider 'Jack' or even 'John' as an acceptable alternative, so Jack is unable to tell her the truth. Lady Bracknell returns to cross-examine Jack about his eligibility as a son-in-law, but rejects him on discovering that he has no known parents but was found as a baby, in a hand-bag, in the cloakroom of Victoria Station in London by a kindly and wealthy old man, who had then adopted him. Disgruntled by events, Jack decides to do away with his fictitious brother, despite Cecily's interest in him. Gwendolen escapes from her mother briefly to vow lasting devotion to her suitor, and asks for his country address, which Algy delightedly notes, resolving to visit Jack's young ward immediately.

Act II
The action moves to the garden terrace of Jack's country house. Cecily, a pretty eighteen-year-old, is being instructed by her governess, Miss Prism, a spinster with fixed ideas about education, literature and morality, and who, it appears, once wrote a sentimental novel but then mislaid the manuscript. Dr Chasuble, an unworldly cleric, lures Miss Prism away for a walk, leaving Cecily alone to welcome a stranger who is announced as 'Ernest Worthing'. Cecily, already enamoured of the name and the reports of Ernest's wickedness, is charmed by the person she meets — it is Algy masquerading as Jack's younger brother. Cecily takes him indoors just before Miss Prism and Dr Chasuble return. They are in time to greet Jack, who is dressed in deep mourning, unaware of the presence of Algy in the guise of young Ernest. Jack announces Ernest's sudden death in Paris and asks Dr Chasuble to rechristen *him* Ernest. He is startled when Cecily enters to break the news of 'Ernest's' arrival, and horrified when Algy appears in this role. However, Jack is unable to unmask his friend without his own deceit being discovered.

Left alone again, Algy and Cecily quickly progress to a declaration of mutual affection, although Algy is disconcerted by Cecily's insistence that a large part of his appeal lies in the name of Ernest. He decides to get baptised as Ernest immediately.

Gwendolen arrives unexpectedly and she and Cecily soon discover that each is engaged to Ernest Worthing; they naturally believe there to be only one. When Jack enters, Gwendolen triumphantly claims him as her Ernest. Cecily corrects her, and then welcomes Algy as *her* Ernest. Gwendolen reveals his true identity. Both girls, united in a sense of outrage, withdraw leaving Algy and Jack to bandy recriminations until Jack orders Algy to leave the house and return to London.

Act III

Cecily and Gwendolen wait in the morning-room, aggrieved that the two men have not tried to pacify them; however, the couples are soon reconciled and a happy ending seems certain until Lady Bracknell appears. She forbids further communication between Jack and Gwendolen, but, reassured by news of Cecily's fortune, gives her consent to Cecily's engagement to Algy. This is opposed by Jack, who, as Cecily's guardian, can prevent the match until she reaches legal maturity at thirty-five. Dr Chasuble arrives, ready to perform the baptisms, but neither of the young men can see any point in continuing. Mention of Miss Prism startles Lady Bracknell. It is revealed that twenty-eight years earlier Miss Prism had been employed by Lady Bracknell but had mysteriously disappeared with the baby boy entrusted to her, leaving behind only the pram and the manuscript of an exceedingly sentimental novel. Miss Prism is summoned and admits, with shame, that she had absent-mindedly left her novel in the pram and deposited the baby, in her black handbag, at Victoria Station. Excitedly Jack produces the handbag in which he was found and claims Miss Prism as his mother. She, a respectable spinster, is shocked by the suggestion and repulses him in horror. Lady Bracknell solves the mystery of Jack's parentage: he is the elder son of her late sister, Mrs Moncrieff, and therefore is Algy's elder brother. The pattern is complete when Jack learns that he was named after his father, General Ernest John Moncrieff. Gwendolen is ecstatic, Algy and Cecily embrace, and even Dr Chasuble and Miss Prism fall into each other's arms. The final exchange between Lady Bracknell and her elder nephew makes the pun in the play's title clear.

> LADY BRACKNELL. My nephew, you seem to be displaying signs of triviality.
> JACK. On the contrary, Aunt Augusta, I've now realised for the first time in my life, the vital Importance of Being Earnest.

In the four-act version, Acts I and II are largely the same, but the middle section of the play is expanded by the introduction of Mr. Gribsby, a solicitor who calls at Jack's country estate to serve a writ for debt against Ernest Worthing. Algy, in his assumed character, protests his innocence and refuses to go quietly off to prison. Gribsby threatens to call in a less genteel Officer of the Court to take Algy — under his alias as Ernest — forcibly to gaol unless the debt of £762 is cleared immediately. Jack, who in his life in Town as Ernest has really incurred the debt, agrees to pay the sum and so the plot continues, as in the shorter version, through comic confusions towards the happy ending.

'The well-made play' and other antecedents

Reviewers of Wilde's earlier plays had commented slightingly on his use of stereotyped or confected plot-lines as mere vehicles for his wit. *The Importance of Being Earnest* was no different. William Archer, for example, noted that 'Incidents of the same nature as Algy Moncrieff's "Bunburying" and John Worthing's invention and subsequent suppression of his scapegrace brother Ernest have done duty in many a French vaudeville or English adaptation.' However, he added: 'But Mr Wilde's humour transmutes them into something entirely new and individual.' (*World*, 20 February 1895) The anonymous critic in *Truth*, 21 February 1895, felt it unnecessary to 'enter into details as to its wildly farcical plot [. . .] as full of echoes as Prospero's isle'. He discovered echoes of W. S. Gilbert and of George Bernard Shaw (1856-1950). Shaw himself was condescending about the play: 'The general effect is that of a farcical comedy dating from the seventies, unplayed during that period because it was too clever and too decent, and brought up to date as far as possible by Mr Wilde in his now completely formed style.' (The *Saturday Review*, 23 February 1895)

Archer's references to French theatre arose from the current fashion for what had been labelled 'well-made plays' and come into the English repertory as adaptations of comedies by dramatists such as Scribe (1791-1861) and Sardou (1831-1908). English playwrights like Henry Arthur Jones (1851-1929) and Sir Arthur Wing Pinero (1855-1934) were developing a recognisable genre with great success in the London theatre, combining the flair for fast-moving and entertaining action seen in the plays of Scribe and Sardou, with a new concern for more serious problems underlying the complacent facade of respectable society, which had been brought into the English theatre recently with the work of the Norwegian dramatist, Henrik Ibsen. Many of Ibsen's plays had been presented in London during the 1880's and 1890's — for example, *A Doll's House* was produced so successfully at the Novelty Theatre in 1889 that it was revived several times. The mechanism of his plays often depends on the idea of the past as a kind of time-bomb ticking ever more loudly beneath the present's surface conventionality until there comes the inevitable explosion and subsequent reassembling of the social fabric. Wilde himself preferred to acknowledge Ibsen as an influence rather than Sardou or Scribe, and there is perhaps some justification for this in a play like *An Ideal Husband* where the issues raised are more serious than questions of the hero's parentage and name.

The 'well-made play' was carefully organised to keep an audience attentive, in a state of suspense, right up to the final dénouement. The construction was obvious and often repeated: background information was given directly through question and answer in the first act (as in *The Importance of Being Earnest*), then the action hurried from one crisis to the next, with coincidence playing a vital part in moving the plot forward should character or situation not provide adequate motivation. Suspense was generated by the audience's knowledge that a secret from the leading character's past (given tangible form as a letter, or a fan, or a jewel, or even a handbag) would disrupt events in the present. Pinero's play, *The Second Mrs Tanqueray,* had proved the popularity of the genre only two years before *The Importance of Being Earnest* made capital out of it while at the same time mocking its conventions. Thus Wilde gives us a 'woman with a past' in the essentially innocent Miss Prism; Jack's guilty secret also demands discovery and is kept dramatically present by the figure of Algy; the black handbag is the key to the truth, revealed only at the last moment.

Wilde's plot was disparagingly described as 'wildly farcical', or, in an unsigned review in *Theatre,* March 1895, as a jumbled collection of 'the elements of farce, comedy and burlesque'. Farce is an exaggerated form of comic drama in which laughter is raised at the expense of probability through an accelerating confusion of events, involving mistaken identities, sudden discoveries of characters in ludicrous or undignified situations, some slapstick comedy — in other words, little subtlety and much hilarious activity. Certainly, the plot of *The Importance of Being Earnest* involves much that is improbable; that two young women should separately determine to love a man called Ernest simply because of his name is unlikely; that Jack should have been found in a handbag by a rich philanthropist and then turn out to be the elder brother of his best friend demands — to use Coleridge's phrase — strenuous 'suspension of disbelief' in the audience. True to the nature of farce, the events move forward with such speed that the audience has little time to examine their improbability. However, *The Importance of Being Earnest* avoids the slapstick elements traditionally associated with farce. Perhaps St. John Hankin described the play best in an article on the *Collected Plays of Oscar Wilde* in the *Fortnightly Review* of May 1908; he called

it 'the farce of ideas'. As for the term 'burlesque', that implies the
mocking through absurdly distorted imitation of some well-known
style of drama or literary fashion. Wilde's play is a burlesque only
in so far as it makes gentle fun of the situations and contrivances
of the fashionable well-made plays of his own time.

Wilde's comic models, however, are older than the nineteenth
century. The device of separating siblings in infancy only to
reunite them just before matrimony goes back at least as far as the
Roman comedies of Terence and Plautus. It also occurs in
Shakespeare's romantic comedies; for example, *The Comedy of
Errors,* itself an adaptation of Plautus, or, in a slightly different
form, *Twelfth Night.* The comic possibilities of a suitor wittily
wooing his mistress under an assumed identity had already been
exploited by Farquhar in *The Beaux' Stratagem* (1707), by
Oliver Goldsmith in *She Stoops to Conquer* (1773) and by Sheridan
in *The Rivals* (1775). The happy ending in which all mysteries
are solved and every character rewarded according to their merits
and the audience's expectations, thanks to the intervention of
Providence or the appearance of a rich and powerful benefactor,
is the very essence of this comic tradition. In *The Rise and Fall of
the Well-Made Play* (London, 1967) John Russell Taylor suggests
that Wilde's skill lay in making the conventional seem exceptional,
particularly in *The Importance of Being Earnest:*

> The plots are creaking old contrivances, and far from trying to
> disguise the fact he glories in it. They are strong enough to hold
> up a glittering display of epigrams, [. . .] and that is all the plot
> is there for. [. . .] The point is that here all the machinery of the
> well-made play finds a triumphantly and unarguably proper use.
> The convention is paramount: nobody really talks or acts like
> this, or certainly not for more than a few moments at a time,
> but, to paraphrase Turner's remark to a lady who objected that
> she never saw sunsets as he painted them, don't we all wish
> they did?

Wilde's wit: the art of paradox and epigram

From the first reviews of his early poetry, through to the obituaries
which attempted to evaluate his life's work, emphasis was placed
on the beauty and wit of Wilde's style. H. G. Wells, writing in the
Daily News in October 1909, argued that behind the apparent
evenness of style there lay a significant variation in quality.

Wilde knew how to say the precise thing which, whether true or false, is irresistible. [. . .] One might go through his swift and sparkling plays with a red and blue pencil marking two kinds of epigrams; the real epigram which he wrote to please his own wild intellect, and the sham epigram he wrote to thrill the very tamest part of our tame civilisation. [. . .] He lowered himself to superiority; he stooped to conquer.

An *epigram* is a balanced statement encapsulating a clever or comic thought. It involves reducing a moral system or a social attitude to a neatly turned phrase. The wit, in the eighteenth-century sense of a creative, cultivated intelligence, is conspicuous. There are many examples of epigram in *The Importance of Being Earnest*, distributed amongst all the characters:

> ALGERNON. More than half of modern culture depends upon what one shouldn't read. (p.5)
> LADY BRACKNELL. Ignorance is like a delicate exotic fruit; touch it and the bloom is gone. (p.17)
> GWENDOLEN. In matters of grave importance, style, not sincerity is the vital thing. (p.58)

These not only have a satisfying cadence, they also contain a variety of attitudes and values within one statement. For instance, Algernon's comment on modern culture can either mean that what was *important* in contemporary literature was censored by 'respectable' Society; or it could imply that what Society hailed as culture was not worth reading. It is the irony implicit in this ambiguity that gives the remark its wit. Wilde's epigrams sometimes made their effect by articulating what many people already knew or believed, winning the laughter of recognition. For example:

> LADY BRACKNELL. Thirty-five is a very attractive age. London society is full of women of the very highest birth who have, of their own free will, remained thirty-five for years. (p.65)

Or:

> ALGERNON. The only way to behave to a woman is to make love to her, if she is pretty, and to some one else, if she is plain. (p.21)

Wilde's *paradoxes* represent a specific style of epigram — that is, the association within one statement of two apparently contradictory ideas in order to challenge accepted conventions or to suggest new ones. Here, too, part of the humour lies in a recognition of the cliché or the convention supporting the paradox. As the Victorian critic, Ernest Newman, argued in *Free Review* (1.6.1895):

> The function of paradox is to illuminate light places, to explain just those things that everyone understands. [. . .] To hear one of Mr Wilde's paradoxes by itself is to be startled; to read them in their proper context is to recognise the great fact on which I have already insisted, that a paradox is a truth seen round a corner.

The audience laughs because the expectations set up in the first part of the statement are overturned by the incongruous or unconventional nature of the second part. For example, 'All women become like their mothers. That is their tragedy' is a conventional kind of mother-in-law joke, still popular with stand-up comedians and writers of comedy sketches. But with his next line Wilde reverses the expected and completes the paradox: 'No man does. That's his.' (p.21)

The humour of paradox and epigram requires an appreciation not only of language's ability to convey truths or to challenge attitudes, but also of the way in which language itself can become absurdly conventional and affected. Wilde sometimes takes a familiar idiom or figure of speech and either reverses its sense or reveals its absurdity. For instance, Algernon complains about the behaviour of married couples in society:

> The amount of women in London who flirt with their own husbands is perfectly scandalous. It looks so bad. It is simply washing one's clean linen in public. (p.9)

The joke lies in Wilde's adaptation of the familiar injunction against washing one's *dirty* linen in public. Algernon's comment has the added strength of conveying succinctly a fashionable attitude to marriage.

Gwendolen scores a point in her verbal duel with Cecily over the ownership of Ernest Worthing by choosing to interpret a figurative cliché literally and so puncture Cecily's air of righteous indignation:

> CECILY. This is no time for wearing the shallow mask of manner. When I see a spade I call it a spade.

> GWENDOLEN. I'm glad to say that I have never seen a spade.
> It is obvious that our social spheres have been widely
> different. (p.48)

More absurdly, Miss Prism explains her use of a common idiom, so
drawing attention to its possible silliness:

> MISS PRISM. Ripeness can be trusted. Young women are
> green. (DR CHASUBLE *starts*.) I spoke horticulturally. My
> metaphor was drawn from fruit. (p.33)

Characters and characterisation

When *The Importance of Being Earnest* was performed a year after
Wilde's death, the critic on the *Sunday Times,* J. T. Grein, stressed
the relevance and the effectiveness of Wilde's social comedy:

> *The Importance of Being Earnest* ranks high, not only on
> account of its gaiety — a gaiety which in many produces the
> smile of intimate understanding, and in the less blasé guffaws
> straight from a happy mood — but because it satirises vividly,
> pointedly, yet not unkindly, the mannerisms and foibles of a
> society which is constantly before the public eye.

'To satirise' means to hold up to ridicule the follies, affectations
or vices of society by presenting the familiar in a slightly unusual
perspective, or by exaggerating certain elements so as to render
the whole grotesque, or at least absurd. Thus **Algernon Moncrieff**,
a pleasant young man of good family and no occupation, displays
quite conventional attitudes and aspirations — a reluctance to
endure domineering relatives, a fondness for food and good
company, a romantic disposition — yet the fecklessness and idleness
of his lifestyle are revealed and ridiculed through his tendency to
reduce every situation or emotion to a neat epigram and to rely
on food to bolster him up at times of stress. He does not differentiate
between matters of serious importance and passing whims; he has
a sentiment pat for every occasion:

> The truth is rarely pure and never simple. Modern life would be
> very tedious if it were either, and modern literature a complete
> impossibility. (p.8)

When the girl he professes to adore apparently rejects him as a
cruel deceiver, he does not beat his breast or weep; he eats muffins.
Wilde not only undercuts any hint of real passion that might have
crept into the courtship scene by making Algy behave so prosaically,

he even underlines the point in the dialogue.

> JACK. How can you sit there, calmly eating muffins when we are in this horrible trouble, I can't make out. You seem to be perfectly heartless.
>
> ALGERNON. Well, I can't eat muffins in an agitated manner. The butter would probably get on my cuffs. One should always eat muffins quite calmly. It is the only way to eat them. (p.54)

That two heroes can be twice as effective as one, particularly in romantic comedy, had already been illustrated in Farquhar's *The Beaux' Stratagem* in which Aimwell and Archer aid and abet each other's country courting; it was also a common pattern in Restoration Comedy; and in *Much Ado About Nothing* Shakespeare used Benedick's lightness of wit to offset Claudio's moodiness. Where the wit consists of the thrust and parry of verbal duelling, a well-matched pair is necessary: Jack and Algernon thus contribute significantly to the play's success through their sparring bouts together, each able to make a witty opening, to parry a cutting epigram and reply with a winning paradox, or pun.

> ALGERNON. Come, old boy, you had much better have the thing out at once.
>
> JACK. My dear Algy, you talk exactly as if you were a dentist. It is very vulgar to talk like a dentist when one isn't a dentist. It produces a false impression.
>
> ALGERNON. Well, that is what dentists always do. (p.7)

Jack parries Algy's demand that he confess everything about 'little Cecily' by concentrating on the pun — or play on words — involved in 'have the thing out' and goes on to make a cutting remark about vulgarity. Algy deflects that thrust by pouncing on the pun implicit in 'It produces a false impression' — it can mean both that 'it gives people a misleading idea' and that 'it imprints an inaccurate shape on a mould such as a dentist might employ when making someone a set of false teeth'.

Two heroes, each pursuing his own desires, also offer occasion for comic plot development, for conflicts of interest, as in Algy's wish to meet Cecily and Jack's determination that he should not. The comic possibilities can be seen when Jack appears at his country home dressed in deep mourning for the death of his fictitious brother Ernest, unaware that Algy has forestalled him by turning up in the guise of young Ernest and being very evidently alive − knowledge that the audience hugs to itself in anticipation of the inevitable confrontation.

Jack Worthing provides a balance to Algy's tireless frivolity; it is he who is required to make a direct connection between the extravagances of the plot and the conventions of real society. He is aware, for example, that being responsible for a rich young girl's education and prospects is a serious business, even if he tries to escape from its weight at times.

> When one is placed in the position of guardian, one has to adopt a very high moral tone on all subjects. It's one's duty to do so. (p.8)

He has every reason for wishing to protect Cecily from anyone who appears as irresponsible and wilful as Algy. When questioned by Lady Bracknell, he is revealed as a conventional and evidently respectable member of society − apart from his inability to produce at least one acceptable parent. The audience at the St. James's Theatre in 1895 would have recognised an income of seven to eight thousand a year, a country estate and a house in Belgrave Square as 'satisfactory', to quote Lady Bracknell. They would also have recognised, as Jack does, Lady Bracknell's right to ask such questions of a prospective son-in-law. What might now appear merely an absurd plot device − the mystery of Jack's parentage − similarly referred to a very real concern in Victorian society about status and a belief in the guarantee of quality endowed upon an individual by a prestigious family tree. It is significant that Jack turns out to have an impeccable pedigree. If he had proved to be the illegitimate son of Miss Prism he would not have been an acceptable match for Gwendolen and the happy ending would have struck a false note.

In his proposal to Gwendolen, Jack loses the wit and confidence of his exchanges with Algy, becoming hesitant and clumsy − suggesting, perhaps, an emotional life beneath the brilliant surface, which Algy never displays.

> JACK. Miss Fairfax, ever since I met you I have admired you more than any girl. . . I have ever met since. . . I met you. (p.13)

His lameness throws her decisiveness into formidable relief:

> GWENDOLEN. Yes, I am quite well aware of the fact. And I often wish that in public, at any rate, you had been more demonstrative. (p.13)

Jack's relative earnestness makes the play less frothy, but Wilde prevents him from becoming too heavy by allowing Algy to parody or deflate his more pompous or sentimental utterances.

> JACK. As for your conduct towards Miss Cardew, I must say that your taking in a sweet, simple, innocent girl like that is quite inexcusable. To say nothing of the fact that she is my ward.
> ALGERNON. I can see no possible defence at all for your deceiving a brilliant, clever, thoroughly experienced young lady like Miss Fairfax. To say nothing of the fact that she is my cousin.
> JACK. I wanted to be engaged to Gwendolen, that is all. I love her.
> ALGERNON. Well, I simply wanted to be engaged to Cecily. I adore her. (p.53)

In terms of the plot, Jack is the focus for the mystery and the first contriver of the intrigues which place this comedy within the tradition of the well-made play. It is his past, contained somehow in the black handbag, which must be revealed before the final curtain; it is his creation of the character of Ernest which leads to the chief complications and dramatic ironies in the action, and it therefore fitting that he should be given the play's last words.

Just as Jack and Algernon are effectively matched, so Gwendolen and Cecily throw each other into comic relief, presenting two traditional views of eligible maidenhood within romantic comedy. **Gwendolen Fairfax**'s confident worldliness and metropolitan hauteur place her in a clear line of descent which reaches back through Congreve's heroine Millamant from *The Way of the World* to one of Shakespeare's sophisticated women, say, Portia from *The Merchant of Venice*. She is aristocratic, opinionated, acknowledged as a beauty, and conscious of being a rich prize. **Cecily Cardew**'s spirited ingenuousness and disconcerting disregard for normal conventions of behaviour, or the candour and spontaneity which make her such a refreshing contrast to the affectations and cynicism of London Society, hark back to Perdita in Shakespeare's *The Winter's Tale* or Miranda in *The Tempest*, or to Kate Hardcastle, the heroine of Goldsmith's comedy *She Stoops to Conquer*, or to Miss Hoyden in Vanbrugh's *The Relapse* (1696).

Gwendolen is evidently her mother's daughter: never at a loss for a word, full of ready-made judgements on all aspects of fashionable life and conventional morality:

> We live, as I hope you know, Mr Worthing, in an age of ideals.
> (p.13)

Or:

> The home seems to me to be the proper sphere for the man.
> And certainly once a man begins to neglect his domestic duties
> he becomes painfully effeminate, does he not? (p.45)

She is intimidating. She reduces Jack to hesitant awkwardness and
ignores Algy altogether. She is humourless, affectedly short-sighted
— because her mother 'whose views on education are remarkably
strict' (p.45) brought her up to be so — and bullyingly dogmatic.
To Cecily she says:

> From the moment I saw you I distrusted you. I felt that you
> were false and deceitful. I am never deceived in such matters.
> My first impressions of people are invariably right. (p.50)

Her rudeness and complacency are funny rather than horrifying
because they do not seem to hurt anyone — Cecily is unimpressed
— and because the audience sees the absurd gap between her idea
of herself and the 'reality'. The remark just quoted becomes
ludicrous in the light of her first speech to Cecily:

> Something tells me that we are going to be great friends. I
> like you already more than I can say. My first impressions of
> people are never wrong. (p.45)

It is important that Gwendolen, like her mother, is apparently
unaware of any inconsistencies or absurdities in her own conduct.
The audience displays its more perfect awareness through laughter.
    Cecily is a successful foil for Algy; she both provokes and
deflates his worldly wit and air of engaging cheerfulness.

> CECILY. Won't you come in?
> ALGERNON. Thank you. Might I have a buttonhole first? I
>   never have any appetite unless I have a buttonhole first.
> CECILY. A Maréchal Niel? (*Picks up scissors.*)
> ALGERNON. No, I'd sooner have a pink rose.
> CECILY. Why? (*Cuts a flower.*)
> ALGERNON. Because you are like a pink rose, Cousin Cecily.
> CECILY. I don't think it can be right for you to talk to me like
>   that. Miss Prism never says such things to me.

ALGERNON. Then Miss Prism is a short-sighted old lady.
(CECILY *puts the rose in his buttonhole.*) You are the
prettiest girl I ever saw.
CECILY. Miss Prism says that all good looks are a snare.
ALGERNON. They are a snare that every sensible man would
like to be caught in.
CECILY. Oh, I don't think I would care to catch a sensible man.
I shouldn't know what to talk to him about. (p.32)

Yet, in her own way she is as formidable as Gwendolen; she takes
the initiative when Algy tries to propose to her (pp.41-44) just as
Gwendolen does with Jack (pp.13-15), displaying at times a
similar incisiveness. When these young women act together they
increase each other's absurdity; for example, at the beginning of
Act III they decide on a dignified silence in the face of Jack's and
Algy's apparent lack of sincerity, then instantly engage the young
men in conversation. They interpret events ludicrously to suit their
own wishes, with no recognition of their silliness. Nonetheless, there
is never any doubt that Gwendolen and Jack (or Ernest, as he
turns out to be) and Cecily and Algernon are 'made for each
other'. The happy ending is both satisfyingly symmetrical and
recognisably right. The couples are well matched in fortune, family
and foolishness.

Lady Bracknell is not a grotesque caricature, in the manner of,
say, the Duchess or the Queen of Hearts in Lewis Carroll's *Alice in
Wonderland;* she behaves with propriety and poise, showing the
same concerns as any conscientious mother in Society — namely
a preoccupation with appearances and a determination to marry
her daughter off brilliantly, or at least presentably. Yet the over-
emphasis on material values, the snobbery, the callousness and
the boorishness of her kind are ridiculed by Wilde. When she hears
that Algy's friend Bunbury is again near death (she has no reason
to suspect that he does not exist), she is merely irritated that her
social arrangements may be unsettled.

Well, I must say, Algernon, that I think it is high time that
Mr Bunbury made up his mind whether he was going to live
or to die. This shilly-shallying with the question is absurd. [. . .]
I should be much obliged if you would ask Mr Bunbury, from
me, to be kind enough not to have a relapse on Saturday, for
I rely on you to arrange my music for me. (p.12)

The humour comes largely from the way Wilde makes her so

forcefully unaware of her own insensitivity and hypocrisy. The audience laughs *at* her not *with* her. When she hears that Jack is unfortunate enough to be an orphan, she shows no sympathy, but there is a kind of incongruous logic in her response:

> To lose one parent, Mr Worthing, may be regarded as a misfortune; to lose both looks like carelessness. (p.18)

She is almost Dickensian: larger than life, absurdly predictable, her character captured in her choice of phrase. However, to complain, as St.John Hankin did, that she and Wilde's other creations have 'no depth, no subtlety' and 'lack solidity', is to mistake Wilde's intention. In a letter to his friend Robert Ross, to whom he dedicated the play, Wilde wrote: 'it has some amusing things in it, and I think the tone and temper of the whole bright and happy'. He described it as 'written by a butterfly for butterflies'. Lady Bracknell may be a dragon, but the lightness and brightness of the whole structure would be overcast if she were allowed to assume the nightmare quality of a really terrifying monster.

A. B. Walkley, writing in the *Spectator* on 23 February 1895, tried to explain where the humour of the characterisation lay:

> Why precisely do we laugh? [. . .] You see that the conduct of the people in itself is rational enough; it is exquisitely irrational in the circumstances. Their motives, too, are quite rational in themselves; they are only irrational as being fitted to the wrong set of actions. And the result is that you have something like real life in detail, yet, in sum, absolutely unlike it.

This comic pattern is visible in the minor characters, too. The governess and the cleric are given a series of set responses — often appropriate enough to the character, yet absurdly inept in the circumstances. The names, as in a Dickens novel, set the tone for the character: **Miss Prism** sounds prim and precise, and **Chasuble**, as well as being the name for a type of priestly vestment, suggests something chaste and cherubic. Miss Prism combines sentimentality with sanctimoniousness:

> Cecily, you will read your Political Economy in my absence. The chapter on the fall of the Rupee you may omit. It is somewhat too sensational. (p.29)

Or:

> The good ended happily, and the bad unhappily. That is what
> Fiction means. (p.28)

Here, of course, the character is unconscious of the humour, unlike
Algy and his studied aphorisms, but the balanced sentence-
structure is of the same quality.

This uniformity of style has been criticised in Wilde's work; for
example, a critic writing in *Truth,* February 1895, complained
that 'there is no attempt in it at characterisation, but all the
dramatis personae, from the heroes down to their butlers, talk
pure and undiluted Wildese'. The *tone* of the remark may alter
to reflect a character's particular degree of self-awareness, but
the symmetry and the comic inversions of conventional patterns
of thought remain constant, sometimes at the expense of a
character's credibility. For instance, Canon Chasuble might appear
inappropriately worldly or cynical in his reply here to Miss Prism:

> MISS PRISM. No married man is ever attractive except to his wife.
> CHASUBLE. And often, I've been told, not even to her. (p.33)

Algy could have delivered that riposte, perhaps, if the inflection
were mocking; Lady Bracknell, too, could have included it
amongst her pronouncements on the ways of her world. Wilde
seems to depend upon the actor to imbue the well-turned phrase
with the necessary ingenuousness in this case. Even a critic such
as William Archer who was enthusiastic about Wilde's plays felt
obliged to point out the danger to Wilde's achievement as a
dramatist of his brilliance as a wit. 'There are times when the
output of Mr Wilde's epigram factory threatens to become all
trademark and no substance.' (*Theatrical World,* 1895) It is
perhaps ironic that as a young man in April 1883 Wilde should
have written to Marie Prescott, an American actress:

> All good dialogue should give the effect of its being made by
> the reaction of the personages on one another. It should never
> seem to be ready made by the author. (*Selected Letters* p.50)

No matter what implausibilities and contrivances may exist in
the plot, nor what some characters may lack in emotional intensity
or psychological detail, *The Importance of Being Earnest* remains
the play for which Oscar Wilde is best remembered. William Archer,
while awake to the play's possible flaws, recognised its vitality
and power to entertain:

It is delightful to see, it sends wave after wave of laughter curling and foaming round the theatre; but as a text for criticism it is barren and delusive. [. . .] What can a poor critic do with a play which raises no principle, whether of art or morals, creates its own canons and conventions, and is nothing but an absolutely wilful expression of an irrepressively witty personality? (*World*, 20 February 1895)

Suggestions for further reading

Collections of Wilde's writings:

Plays, Prose Writings, and Poems (London, Dent: Everyman's Library)
  Contains *Importance* and *Lady Windermere's Fan* as well as *The Picture of Dorian Gray, The Ballad of Reading Gaol* and the essays 'The Critic as Artist' and 'The Soul of Man Under Socialism'.

Three Plays (London, Eyre Methuen: Master Playwrights)
  Contains *An Ideal Husband* and *Lady Windermere's Fan* as well as *Importance* with additional material from the Fourth Act. Introduction by H. Montgomery Hyde.

Portable Oscar Wilde (Harmondsworth, Penguin: Viking Portable Library).

De Profundis (Harmondsworth, Penguin: Penguin English Library).

Lord Arthur Savile's Crime and Other Stories (Harmondsworth, Penguin: Modern Classics).

General biographical background

Oscar Wilde by H. Montgomery Hyde (London, Eyre Methuen and Magnum)

Selected Letters of Oscar Wilde, edited by Rupert Hart-Davis (Oxford University Press)

Son of Oscar Wilde by Vyvyan Holland (London, Hart-Davis).

General critical studies

Oscar Wilde by James Laver (British Council).

Oscar Wilde: A Collection of Critical Essays, edited by Richard Ellmann (Englewood Cliffs, Prentice-Hall).

Articles on specific aspects of the play

James M. Ware, 'Algernon's Appetite: Oscar Wilde's Hero as Restoration Dandy', *English Literature in Transition,* 13. 1, 1970, pp.17-26.

John Gielguid, essay in *Stage Directions* (London, Heinemann) pp.78-84.

David Parker, 'Oscar Wilde's Great Farce', *Modern Language Quarterly*, 35, June 1974, pp.173-186.

Paul C. Wadleigh, '*Earnest* at St James's Theatre', *Quarterly Journal of Speech*, 52, 1966, pp.59-62.

Joseph W. Donahue, 'The First Production of *Importance:* Proposal for a Reconstructive Study', in *Essays on 19th Century British Theatre,* edited by Kenneth Richards and Peter Thomson (London, Methuen).

George Alexander (*above*), the original Jack Worthing, 1895. *Below:* Algernon, Cecily, Jack, Prism and Chasuble in the 1923 Haymarket production, the last to be played in 'modern dress' as opposed to period costume. (Photos: Mander & Mitchenson)

Gwendolen and Jack surprised by Lady Bracknell (Act I). *Above*: in 1909.
Below: in 1942, John Gielgud as Jack, Edith Evans as Lady B. (Photos:
Mander & Mitchenson) *Right*: in the 1952 film, Michael Redgrave as Jack,
Joan Greenwood as Gwendolen. (EMI)

Above: the cucumber sandwiches — Jack and Algernon (Michael Denison).
Below: Miss Prism (Margaret Rutherford), Canon Chasuble (Miles Malleson) and Cecily (Dorothy Tutin) Act II. (Both from the film: EMI)

Above: Algernon, Merriman and Jack, 'in the deepest mourning' (Act II).
Below: Gwendolen examining Cecily through her lorgnette (Act II).
(Both from the film: EMI)

Above: Lady Bracknell (Edith Evans) interviewing Jack (Act III). *Below*: 'Mother!' — Jack and Miss Prism (Act III). (Both from the film: EMI)

The Importance of
Being Earnest

The Importance of Being Earnest was first performed at the St James Theatre, London on 14th February, 1895, with the following cast:

JOHN WORTHING, J.P.	Mr George Alexander
ALGERNON MONCRIEFF	Mr Allen Aynesworth
REV. CANON CHASUBLE, D.D.	Mr H. H. Vincent
MERRIMAN (Butler)	Mr Frank Dyall
LANE (Manservant)	Mr F. Kinsey Peile
LADY BRACKNELL	Miss Rose Leclercq
HON. GWENDOLEN FAIRFAX	Miss Irene Vanbrugh
CECILY CARDEW	Miss Evelyn Millard
MISS PRISM (Governess)	Mrs George Canninge

Lessee and Manager: Mr George Alexander

THE SCENES OF THE PLAY

ACT I   Algernon Moncrieff's Flat in Half-Moon Street, W.

ACT II   The Garden at the Manor House, Woolton.

ACT III   Drawing-Room at the Manor House, Woolton.

TIME: The Present

First Act

Morning-room in Algernon's flat in Half-Moon Street. The room is luxuriously and artistically furnished. The sound of a piano is heard in the adjoining room.

LANE *is arranging afternoon tea on the table, and after the music has ceased,* ALGERNON *enters.*

ALGERNON. Did you hear what I was playing, Lane?

LANE. I didn't think it polite to listen, sir.

ALGERNON. I'm sorry for that, for your sake. I don't play accurately – any one can play accurately – but I play with wonderful expression. As far as the piano is concerned, sentiment is my forte. I keep science for Life.

LANE. Yes, sir.

ALGERNON. And, speaking of the science of Life, have you got the cucumber sandwiches cut for Lady Bracknell?

LANE. Yes, sir. (*Hands them on a salver.*)

ALGERNON (*inspects them, takes two, and sits down on the sofa*). Oh! . . . by the way, Lane, I see from your book that on Thursday night, when Lord Shoreman and Mr Worthing were dining with me, eight bottles of champagne are entered as having been consumed.

LANE. Yes, sir; eight bottles and a pint.

ALGERNON. Why is it that at a bachelor's establishment the servants invariably drink the champagne? I ask merely for information.

LANE. I attribute it to the superior quality of the wine, sir. I have often observed that in married households the champagne is rarely of a first-rate brand.

ALGERNON. Good heavens! Is marriage so demoralising as that?

LANE. I believe it *is* a very pleasant state, sir. I have had very little experience of it myself up to the present. I have only been married once. That was in consequence of a misunderstanding between myself and a young person.

ALGERNON (*languidly*). I don't know that I am much interested in your family life, Lane.

LANE. No, sir; it is not a very interesting subject. I never think of it myself.

ALGERNON. Very natural, I am sure. That will do, Lane, thank you.

LANE. Thank you, sir.

LANE goes out.

ALGERNON. Lane's views on marriage seem somewhat lax. Really, if the lower orders don't set us a good example, what on earth is the use of them? They seem, as a class, to have absolutely no sense of moral responsibility.

Enter LANE.

LANE. Mr Ernest Worthing.

Enter JACK.

LANE goes out.

ALGERNON. How are you, my dear Ernest? What brings you up to town?

JACK. Oh, pleasure, pleasure! What else should bring one anywhere? Eating as usual, I see, Algy!

ALGERNON (*stiffly*). I believe it is customary in good society to take some slight refreshment at five o'clock. Where have you been since last Thursday?

JACK (*sitting down on the sofa*). In the country.

ALGERNON. What on earth do you do there?

JACK (*pulling off his gloves*). When one is in town one amuses oneself. When one is in the country one amuses other people. It is excessively boring.

ALGERNON. And who are the people you amuse?

JACK (*airily*). Oh, neighbours, neighbours.

ALGERNON. Got nice neighbours in your part of Shropshire?

JACK. Perfectly horrid! Never speak to one of them.

ALGERNON. How immensely you must amuse them! (*Goes over and takes sandwich.*) By the way, Shropshire is your county, is it not?

JACK. Eh? Shropshire? Yes, of course. Hallo! Why all these cups? Why cucumber sandwiches? Why such reckless extravagance in one so young? Who is coming to tea?

ALGERNON. Oh! merely Aunt Augusta and Gwendolen.

JACK. How perfectly delightful!

ALGERNON. Yes, that is all very well; but I am afraid Aunt Augusta won't quite approve of your being here.

JACK. May I ask why?

ALGERNON. My dear fellow, the way you flirt with Gwendolen is perfectly disgraceful. It is almost as bad as the way Gwendolen flirts with you.

JACK. I am in love with Gwendolen. I have come up to town expressly to propose to her.

ALGERNON. I thought you had come up for pleasure? . . . I call that business.

JACK. How utterly unromantic you are!

ALGERNON. I really don't see anything romantic in proposing. It is very romantic to be in love. But there is nothing romantic about a definite proposal. Why, one may be accepted. One usually is, I believe. Then the excitement is all over. The very essence of romance is uncertainty. If ever I get married, I'll certainly try to forget the fact.

JACK. I have no doubt about that, dear Algy. The Divorce

Court was specially invented for people whose memories are
so curiously constituted.

ALGERNON. Oh! there is no use speculating on that subject.
Divorces are made in Heaven — (JACK *puts out his hand to
take a sandwich.* ALGERNON *at once interferes.*) Please don't
touch the cucumber sandwiches. They are ordered specially
for Aunt Augusta. (*Takes one and eats it.*)

JACK. Well, you have been eating them all the time.

ALGERNON. That is quite a different matter. She is my aunt.
(*Takes plate from below.*) Have some bread and butter. The
bread and butter is for Gwendolen. Gwendolen is devoted to
bread and butter.

JACK (*advancing to table and helping himself*). And very good
bread and butter it is too.

ALGERNON. Well, my dear fellow, you need not eat as if you
were going to eat it all. You behave as if you were married to
her already. You are not married to her already, and I don't
think you ever will be.

JACK. Why on earth do you say that?

ALGERNON. Well, in the first place girls never marry the men
they flirt with. Girls don't think it right.

JACK. Oh, that is nonsense!

ALGERNON. It isn't. It is a great truth. It accounts for the
extraordinary number of bachelors that one sees all over the
place. In the second place, I don't give my consent.

JACK. Your consent!

ALGERNON. My dear fellow, Gwendolen is my first cousin.
And before I allow you to marry her, you will have to clear
up the whole question of Cecily. (*Rings bell.*)

JACK. Cecily! What on earth do you mean? What do you mean,
Algy, by Cecily! I don't know any one of the name of Cecily.

Enter LANE.

ALGERNON. Bring me that cigarette case Mr Worthing left in
the smoking-room the last time he dined here.

LANE. Yes, sir.

LANE goes out.

JACK. Do you mean to say you have had my cigarette case all this time? I wish to goodness you had let me know. I have been writing frantic letters to Scotland Yard about it. I was very nearly offering a large reward.

ALGERNON. Well, I wish you would offer one. I happen to be more than usually hard up.

JACK. There is no good offering a large reward now that the thing is found.

Enter LANE *with the cigarette case on a salver.* ALGERNON *takes it at once.* LANE *goes out.*

ALGERNON. I think that is rather mean of you, Ernest, I must say. (*Opens case and examines it.*) However, it makes no matter, for, now that I look at the inscription inside, I find that the thing isn't yours after all.

JACK. Of course it's mine. (*Moving to him.*) You have seen me with it a hundred times, and you have no right whatsoever to read what is written inside. It is a very ungentlemanly thing to read a private cigarette case.

ALGERNON. Oh! it is absurd to have a hard and fast rule about what one should read and what one shouldn't. More than half of modern culture depends on what one shouldn't read.

JACK. I am quite aware of the fact, and I don't propose to discuss modern culture. It isn't the sort of thing one should talk of in private. I simply want my cigarette case back.

ALGERNON. Yes; but this isn't your cigarette case. This cigarette case is a present from some one of the name of Cecily, and you said you didn't know any one of that name.

JACK. Well, if you want to know, Cecily happens to be my aunt.

ALGERNON. Your aunt!

JACK. Yes. Charming old lady she is, too. Lives at Tunbridge Wells. Just give it back to me, Algy.

ALGERNON (*retreating to back of sofa*). But why does she call herself little Cecily if she is your aunt and lives at Tunbridge Wells? (*Reading*.) 'From little Cecily with her fondest love.'

JACK (*moving to sofa and kneeling upon it*). My dear fellow, what on earth is there in that? Some aunts are tall, some aunts are not tall. That is a matter that surely an aunt may be allowed to decide for herself. You seem to think that every aunt should be exactly like your aunt! That is absurd! For Heaven's sake give me back my cigarette case. (*Follows* ALGERNON *round the room*.)

ALGERNON. Yes. But why does your aunt call you her uncle? 'From little Cecily, with her fondest love to her dear Uncle Jack.' There is no objection, I admit, to an aunt being a small aunt, but why an aunt, no matter what her size may be, should call her own nephew her uncle, I can't quite make out. Besides, your name isn't Jack at all; it is Ernest.

JACK. It isn't Ernest; it's Jack.

ALGERNON. You have always told me it was Ernest. I have introduced you to every one as Ernest. You answer to the name of Ernest. You look as if your name was Ernest. You are the most earnest-looking person I ever saw in my life. It is perfectly absurd your saying that your name isn't Ernest. It's on your cards. Here is one of them. (*Taking it from case*.) 'Mr Ernest Worthing, B. 4, The Albany.' I'll keep this as a proof that your name is Ernest if ever you attempt to deny it to me, or to Gwendolen, or to any one else. (*Puts the card in his pocket*.)

JACK. Well, my name is Ernest in town and Jack in the country, and the cigarette case was given to me in the country.

ALGERNON. Yes, but that does not account for the fact that your small Aunt Cecily, who lives at Tunbridge Wells, calls you her dear uncle. Come, old boy, you had much better have the thing out at once.

JACK. My dear Algy, you talk exactly as if you were a dentist. It is very vulgar to talk like a dentist when one isn't a dentist. It produces a false impression.

ALGERNON. Well, that is exactly what dentists always do. Now, go on! Tell me the whole thing. I may mention that I have always suspected you of being a confirmed and secret Bunburyist; and I am quite sure of it now.

JACK. Bunburyist? What on earth do you mean by a Bunburyist?

ALGERNON. I'll reveal to you the meaning of that incomparable expression as soon as you are kind enough to inform me why you are Ernest in town and Jack in the country.

JACK. Well, produce my cigarette case first.

ALGERNON. Here it is. (*Hands cigarette case.*) Now produce your explanation, and pray make it improbable. (*Sits on sofa.*)

JACK. My dear fellow, there is nothing improbable about my explanation at all. In fact it's perfectly ordinary. Old Mr Thomas Cardew, who adopted me when I was a little boy, made me in his will guardian to his grand-daughter, Miss Cecily Cardew. Cecily, who addresses me as her uncle from motives of respect that you could not possibly appreciate, lives at my place in the country under the charge of her admirable governess, Miss Prism.

ALGERNON. Where is that place in the country, by the way?

JACK. That is nothing to you, dear boy. You are not going to be invited. . . . I may tell you candidly that the place is not in Shropshire.

ALGERNON. I suspected that, my dear fellow! I have Bunburyed all over Shropshire on two separate occasions. Now, go on. Why are you Ernest in town and Jack in the country?

JACK. My dear Algy, I don't know whether you will be able to understand my real motives. You are hardly serious enough.

When one is placed in the position of guardian, one has to adopt a very high moral tone on all subjects. It's one's duty to do so. And as a high moral tone can hardly be said to conduce very much to either one's health or one's happiness, in order to get up to town I have always pretended to have a younger brother of the name of Ernest, who lives in the Albany, and gets into the most dreadful scrapes. That, my dear Algy, is the whole truth pure and simple.

ALGERNON. The truth is rarely pure and never simple. Modern life would be very tedious if it were either, and modern literature a complete impossibility!

JACK. That wouldn't be at all a bad thing.

ALGERNON. Literary criticism is not your forte, my dear fellow. Don't try it. You should leave that to people who haven't been at a University. They do it so well in the daily papers. What you really are is a Bunburyist. I was quite right in saying you were a Bunburyist. You are one of the most advanced Bunburyists I know.

JACK. What on earth do you mean?

ALGERNON. You have invented a very useful younger brother called Ernest, in order that you may be able to come up to town as often as you like. I have invented an invaluable permanent invalid called Bunbury, in order that I may be able to go down into the country whenever I choose. Bunbury is perfectly invaluable. If it wasn't for Bunbury's extraordinary bad health, for instance, I wouldn't be able to dine with you at Willis's to-night, for I have been really engaged to Aunt Augusta for more than a week.

JACK. I haven't asked you to dine with me anywhere to-night.

ALGERNON. I know. You are absurdly careless about sending out invitations. It is very foolish of you. Nothing annoys people so much as not receiving invitations.

JACK. You had much better dine with your Aunt Augusta.

ALGERNON. I haven't the smallest intention of doing anything of the kind. To begin with, I dined there on Monday, and once a week is quite enough to dine with one's own relations. In the second place, whenever I do dine there I am always treated as a member of the family, and sent down with either no woman at all, or two. In the third place, I know perfectly well whom she will place me next to, to-night. She will place me next to Mary Farquhar, who always flirts with her own husband across the dinner-table. That is not very pleasant. Indeed, it is not even decent . . . and that sort of thing is enormously on the increase. The amount of women in London who flirt with their own husbands is perfectly scandalous. It looks so bad. It is simply washing one's clean linen in public. Besides, now that I know you to be a confirmed Bunburyist I naturally want to talk to you about Bunburying. I want to tell you the rules.

JACK. I'm not a Bunburyist at all. If Gwendolen accepts me, I am going to kill my brother, indeed I think I'll kill him in any case. Cecily is a little too much interested in him. It is rather a bore. So I am going to get rid of Ernest. And I strongly advise you to do the same with Mr. . . . with your invalid friend who has the absurd name.

ALGERNON. Nothing will induce me to part with Bunbury, and if you ever get married, which seems to me extremely problematic, you will be very glad to know Bunbury. A man who marries without knowing Bunbury has a very tedious time of it.

JACK. That is nonsense. If I marry a charming girl like Gwendolen, and she is the only girl I ever saw in my life that I would marry, I certainly won't want to know Bunbury.

ALGERNON. Then your wife will. You don't seem to realise, that in married life three is company and two is none.

JACK (*sententiously*). That, my dear young friend, is the theory that the corrupt French Drama has been propounding for the last fifty years.

ALGERNON. Yes; and that the happy English home has proved in half the time.

JACK. For heaven's sake, don't try to be cynical. It's perfectly easy to be cynical.

ALGERNON. My dear fellow, it isn't easy to be anything nowa-days. There's such a lot of beastly competition about. (*The sound of an electric bell is heard.*) Ah! that must be Aunt Augusta. Only relatives, or creditors, ever ring in that Wagnerian manner. Now, if I get her out of the way for ten minutes, so that you can have an opportunity for proposing to Gwendolen, may I dine with you to-night at Willis's?

JACK. I suppose so, if you want to.

ALGERNON. Yes, but you must be serious about it. I hate people who are not serious about meals. It is so shallow of them.

Enter LANE.

LANE. Lady Bracknell and Miss Fairfax.

ALGERNON *goes forward to meet them. Enter* LADY BRACKNELL *and* GWENDOLEN.

LADY BRACKNELL. Good afternoon, dear Algernon, I hope you are behaving very well.

ALGERNON. I'm feeling very well, Aunt Augusta.

LADY BRACKNELL. That's not quite the same thing. In fact the two things rarely go together. (*Sees* JACK *and bows to him with icy coldness.*)

ALGERNON (*To* GWENDOLEN). Dear me, you are smart!

GWENDOLEN. I am always smart! Am I not, Mr Worthing?

JACK. You're quite perfect, Miss Fairfax.

GWENDOLEN. Oh! I hope I am not that. It would leave no room for developments, and I intend to develop in many directions. (GWENDOLEN *and* JACK *sit down together in the corner.*)

LADY BRACKNELL. I'm sorry if we are a little late, Algernon, but I was obliged to call on dear Lady Harbury. I hadn't been there since her poor husband's death. I never saw a woman so altered; she looks quite twenty years younger. And now I'll have a cup of tea, and one of those nice cucumber sandwiches you promised me.

ALGERNON. Certainly, Aunt Augusta. (*Goes over to tea-table*).

LADY BRACKNELL. Won't you come and sit here, Gwendolen?

GWENDOLEN. Thanks, mamma, I'm quite comfortable where I am.

ALGERNON (*picking up empty plate in horror*). Good heavens! Lane! Why are there no cucumber sandwiches? I ordered them specially.

LANE (*gravely*). There were no cucumbers in the market this morning, sir. I went down twice.

ALGERNON. No cucumbers!

LANE. No, sir. Not even for ready money.

ALGERNON. That will do, Lane, thank you.

LANE. Thank you, sir.

Goes out.

ALGERNON. I am greatly distressed, Aunt Augusta, about there being no cucumbers, not even for ready money.

LADY BRACKNELL. It really makes no matter, Algernon. I had some crumpets with Lady Harbury, who seems to me to be living entirely for pleasure now.

ALGERNON. I hear her hair has turned quite gold from grief.

LADY BRACKNELL. It certainly has changed its colour. From what cause I, of course, cannot say. (ALGERNON *crosses and hands tea.*) Thank you. I've quite a treat for you to-night, Algernon. I am going to send you down with Mary Farquhar. She is such a nice woman, and so attentive to her husband. It's delightful to watch them.

ALGERNON. I am afraid, Aunt Augusta, I shall have to give up the pleasure of dining with you to-night after all.

LADY BRACKNELL (*frowning*). I hope not, Algernon. It would

put my table completely out. Your uncle would have to dine upstairs. Fortunately he is accustomed to that.

ALGERNON. It is a great bore, and, I need hardly say, a terrible disappointment to me, but the fact is I have just had a telegram to say that my poor friend Bunbury is very ill again. (*Exchanges glances with* JACK.) They seem to think I should be with him.

LADY BRACKNELL. It is very strange. This Mr Bunbury seems to suffer from curiously bad health.

ALGERNON. Yes; poor Bunbury is a dreadful invalid.

LADY BRACKNELL. Well, I must say, Algernon, that I think it is high time that Mr Bunbury made up his mind whether he was going to live or to die. This shilly-shallying with the question is absurd. Nor do I in any way approve of the modern sympathy with invalids. I consider it morbid. Illness of any kind is hardly a thing to be encouraged in others. Health is the primary duty of life. I am always telling that to your poor uncle, but he never seems to take much notice . . . as far as any improvement in his ailment goes. I should be much obliged if you would ask Mr Bunbury, from me, to be kind enough not to have a relapse on Saturday, for I rely on you to arrange my music for me. It is my last reception, and one wants something that will encourage conversation, particularly at the end of the season when every one has practically said whatever they had to say, which, in most cases, was probably not much.

ALGERNON. I'll speak to Bunbury, Aunt Augusta, if he is still conscious, and I think I can promise you he'll be all right by Saturday. Of course the music is a great difficulty. You see, if one plays good music, people don't listen, and if one plays bad music people don't talk. But I'll run over the programme I've drawn out, if you will kindly come into the next room for a moment.

LADY BRACKNELL. Thank you, Algernon. It is very thoughtful of you. (*Rising, and following* ALGERNON.) I'm sure the programme will be delightful, after a few expurgations. French songs I cannot possibly allow. People always seem to think that they are improper, and either look shocked, which is vulgar, or laugh, which is worse. But German sounds a thoroughly respectable language, and indeed, I believe is so. Gwendolen, you will accompany me.

GWENDOLEN. Certainly, mamma.

> LADY BRACKNELL *and* ALGERNON *go into the music-room,* GWENDOLEN *remains behind.*

JACK. Charming day it has been, Miss Fairfax.

GWENDOLEN. Pray don't talk to me about the weather, Mr Worthing. Whenever people talk to me about the weather, I always feel quite certain that they mean something else. And that makes me so nervous.

JACK. I do mean something else.

GWENDOLEN. I thought so. In fact, I am never wrong.

JACK. And I would like to be allowed to take advantage of Lady Bracknell's temporary absence . . .

GWENDOLEN. I would certainly advise you to do so. Mamma has a way of coming back suddenly into a room that I have often had to speak to her about.

JACK (*nervously*). Miss Fairfax, ever since I met you I have admired you more than any girl . . . I have ever met since . . . I met you.

GWENDOLEN. Yes, I am quite well aware of the fact. And I often wish that in public, at any rate, you had been more demonstrative. For me you have always had an irresistible fascination. Even before I met you I was far from indifferent to you. (JACK *looks at her in amazement.*) We live, as I hope you know, Mr Worthing, in an age of ideals. The fact is constantly mentioned in the more expensive monthly magazines, and has reached the provincial pulpits, I am told; and my ideal has always been to love some one of the name of Ernest. There is something in that name that inspires absolute confidence. The moment Algernon first mentioned to me that he had a friend called Ernest, I knew I was destined to love you.

JACK. You really love me, Gwendolen?

GWENDOLEN. Passionately!

JACK. Darling! You don't know how happy you've made me.

GWENDOLEN. My own Ernest!

JACK. But you don't really mean to say that you couldn't love me if my name wasn't Ernest?

GWENDOLEN. But your name is Ernest.

JACK. Yes, I know it is. But supposing it was something else? Do you mean to say you couldn't love me then?

GWENDOLEN (*glibly*). Ah! that is clearly a metaphysical speculation, and like most metaphysical speculations has very little reference at all to the actual facts of real life, as we know them.

JACK. Personally, darling, to speak quite candidly, I don't much care about the name of Ernest. . . . I don't think the name suits me at all.

GWENDOLEN. It suits you perfectly. It is a divine name. It has music of its own. It produces vibrations.

JACK. Well, really, Gwendolen, I must say that I think there are lots of other much nicer names. I think Jack, for instance, a charming name.

GWENDOLEN. Jack? . . . No, there is very little music in the name Jack, if any at all, indeed. It does not thrill. It produces absolutely no vibrations. . . . I have known several Jacks, and they all, without exception, were more than usually plain. Besides, Jack is a notorious domesticity for John! And I pity any woman who is married to a man called John. She would probably never be allowed to know the entrancing pleasure of a single moment's solitude. The only really safe name is Ernest.

JACK. Gwendolen, I must get christened at once—I mean we must get married at once. There is no time to be lost.

GWENDOLEN. Married, Mr Worthing?

JACK (*astounded*). Well . . . surely. You know that I love you, and you led me to believe, Miss Fairfax, that you were not absolutely indifferent to me.

GWENDOLEN. I adore you. But you haven't proposed to me yet. Nothing has been said at all about marriage. The subject has not even been touched on.

JACK. Well . . . may I propose to you now?

GWENDOLEN. I think it would be an admirable opportunity. And to spare you any possible disappointment, Mr Worthing, I think it only fair to tell you quite frankly beforehand that I am fully determined to accept you.

JACK. Gwendolen!

GWENDOLEN. Yes, Mr Worthing, what have you got to say to me?

JACK. You know what I have got to say to you.

GWENDOLEN. Yes, but you don't say it.

JACK. Gwendolen, will you marry me? (*Goes on his knees.*)

GWENDOLEN. Of course I will, darling. How long you have been about it! I am afraid you have had very little experience in how to propose.

JACK. My own one, I have never loved any one in the world but you.

GWENDOLEN. Yes, but men often propose for practice. I know my brother Gerald does. All my girl-friends tell me so. What wonderfully blue eyes you have, Ernest! They are quite, quite, blue. I hope you will always look at me just like that, especially when there are other people present.

Enter LADY BRACKNELL.

LADY BRACKNELL. Mr Worthing! Rise, sir, from this semi-recumbent posture. It is most indecorous.

GWENDOLEN. Mamma! (*He tries to rise; she restrains him.*) I must beg you to retire. This is no place for you. Besides, Mr Worthing has not quite finished yet.

LADY BRACKNELL. Finished what, may I ask?

GWENDOLEN. I am engaged to Mr. Worthing, mamma. (*They rise together*).

LADY BRACKNELL. Pardon me, you are not engaged to any one. When you do become engaged to some one, I, or your father, should his health permit him, will inform you of the fact. An engagement should come on a young girl as a surprise, pleasant or unpleasant, as the case may be. It is hardly a matter that she could be allowed to arrange for herself. . . . And now I have a few questions to put to you, Mr Worthing. While I am making these inquiries, you, Gwendolen, will wait for me below in the carriage.

GWENDOLEN (*reproachfully*). Mamma!

LADY BRACKNELL. In the carriage, Gwendolen! (GWENDOLEN *goes to the door. She and* JACK *blow kisses to each other behind* LADY BRACKNELL'S *back.* LADY BRACKNELL *looks vaguely about as if she could not understand what the noise was. Finally turns round.*) Gwendolen, the carriage!

GWENDOLEN. Yes, mamma. (*Goes out, looking back at* JACK.)

LADY BRACKNELL (*sitting down*). You can take a seat, Mr Worthing.

Looks in her pocket for note-book and pencil.

JACK. Thank you, Lady Bracknell, I prefer standing.

LADY BRACKNELL (*pencil and note-book in hand*). I feel bound to tell you that you are not down on my list of eligible young men, although I have the same list as the dear Duchess of Bolton has. We work together, in fact. However, I am quite ready to enter your name, should your answers be what a really affectionate mother requires. Do you smoke?

JACK. Well, yes, I must admit I smoke.

LADY BRACKNELL. I am glad to hear it. A man should always have an occupation of some kind. There are far too many idle men in London as it is. How old are you?

JACK. Twenty-nine.

LADY BRACKNELL. A very good age to be married at. I have always been of opinion that a man who desires to get married should know either everything or nothing. Which do you know?

JACK (*after some hesitation*). I know nothing, Lady Bracknell.

LADY BRACKNELL. I am pleased to hear it. I do not approve of anything that tampers with natural ignorance. Ignorance is like a delicate exotic fruit; touch it and the bloom is gone. The whole theory of modern education is radically unsound. Fortunately in England, at any rate, education produces no effect whatsoever. If it did, it would prove a serious danger to the upper classes, and probably lead to acts of violence in Grosvenor Square. What is your income?

JACK. Between seven and eight thousand a year.

LADY BRACKNELL (*makes a note in her book*). In land, or in investments?

JACK. In investments, chiefly.

LADY BRACKNELL. That is satisfactory. What between the duties expected of one during one's lifetime, and the duties exacted from one after one's death, land has ceased to be either a profit or a pleasure. It gives one position, and prevents one from keeping it up. That's all that can be said about land.

JACK. I have a country house with some land, of course, attached to it, about fifteen hundred acres, I believe; but I don't depend on that for my real income. In fact, as far as I can make out, the poachers are the only people who make anything out of it.

LADY BRACKNELL. A country house! How many bedrooms? Well, that point can be cleared up afterwards. You have a town house, I hope? A girl with a simple, unspoiled nature, like Gwendolen, could hardly be expected to reside in the country.

JACK. Well, I own a house in Belgrave Square, but it is let by

the year to Lady Bloxham. Of course, I can get it back whenever I like, at six months' notice.

LADY BRACKNELL. Lady Bloxham? I don't know her.

JACK. Oh, she goes about very little. She is a lady considerably
advanced in years.

LADY BRACKNELL. Ah, nowadays that is no guarantee of
respectability of character. What number in Belgrave Square?

JACK. 149.

LADY BRACKNELL (*shaking her head*). The unfashionable side.
I thought there was something. However, that could easily
be altered.

JACK. Do you mean the fashion, or the side?

LADY BRACKNELL (*sternly*). Both, if necessary, I presume.
What are your politics?

JACK. Well, I am afraid I really have none. I am a Liberal
Unionist.

LADY BRACKNELL. Oh, they count as Tories. They dine with
us. Or come in the evening, at any rate. Now to minor
matters. Are your parents living?

JACK. I have lost both my parents.

LADY BRACKNELL. To lose one parent, Mr Worthing, may
be regarded as a misfortune; to lose both looks like careless-
ness. Who was your father? He was evidently a man of some
wealth. Was he born in what the Radical papers call the
purple of commerce, or did he rise from the ranks of the
aristocracy?

JACK. I am afraid I really don't know. The fact is, Lady
Bracknell, I said I had lost my parents. It would be nearer
the truth to say that my parents seem to have lost me. . . .
I don't actually know who I am by birth. I was . . . well, I
was found.

LADY BRACKNELL. Found!

JACK. The late Mr Thomas Cardew, an old gentleman of a
very charitable and kindly disposition, found me, and gave
me the name of Worthing, because he happened to have a

first-class ticket for Worthing in his pocket at the time.
Worthing is a place in Sussex. It is a seaside resort.

LADY BRACKNELL. Where did the charitable gentleman who
had a first-class ticket for this seaside resort find you?

JACK (*gravely*). In a hand-bag.

LADY BRACKNELL. A hand-bag?

JACK (*very seriously*). Yes, Lady Bracknell. I was in a hand-bag
– a somewhat large, black leather hand-bag, with handles to
it – an ordinary hand-bag in fact.

LADY BRACKNELL. In what locality did this Mr James, or
Thomas, Cardew come across this ordinary hand-bag?

JACK. In the cloak-room at Victoria Station. It was given to
him in mistake for his own.

LADY BRACKNELL. The cloakroom at Victoria Station?

JACK. Yes. The Brighton line.

LADY BRACKNELL. The line is immaterial. Mr Worthing, I
confess I feel somewhat bewildered by what you have just
told me. To be born, or at any rate bred, in a hand-bag,
whether it had handles or not, seems to me to display a
contempt for the ordinary decencies of family life that
reminds one of the worst excesses of the French Revolution.
And I presume you know what that unfortunate movement
led to? As for the particular locality in which the hand-bag
was found, a cloak-room at a railway station might serve to
conceal a social indiscretion – has probably, indeed, been
used for that purpose before now – but it could hardly be
regarded as an assured basis for a recognised position in good
society.

JACK. May I ask you then what you would advise me to do?
I need hardly say I would do anything in the world to ensure
Gwendolen's happiness.

LADY BRACKNELL. I would strongly advise you, Mr Worthing, to try and acquire some relations as soon as possible,
and to make a definite effort to produce at any rate one
parent, of either sex, before the season is quite over.

JACK. Well, I don't see how I could possibly manage to do that. I can produce the hand-bag at any moment. It is in my dressing-room at home. I really think that should satisfy you, Lady Bracknell.

LADY BRACKNELL. Me, Sir! What has it to do with me? You can hardly imagine that I and Lord Bracknell would dream of allowing our only daughter – a girl brought up with the utmost care – to marry into a cloak-room, and form an alliance with a parcel? Good morning, Mr. Worthing!

LADY BRACKNELL sweeps out in majestic indignation.

JACK. Good morning! (ALGERNON, *from the other room, strikes up the Wedding March.* JACK *looks perfectly furious, and goes to the door.*) For goodness' sake don't play that ghastly tune, Algy! How idiotic you are!

The music stops and ALGERNON *enters cheerily.*

ALGERNON. Didn't it go off all right, old boy? You don't mean to say Gwendolen refused you? I know it is a way she has. She is always refusing people. I think it is most ill-natured of her.

JACK. Oh, Gwendolen is as right as a trivet. As far as she is concerned, we are engaged. Her mother is perfectly unbearable. Never met such a Gorgon. . . . I don't really know what a Gorgon is like, but I am quite sure that Lady Bracknell is one. In any case, she is a monster, without being a myth, which is rather unfair. . . . I beg your pardon, Algy, I suppose I shouldn't talk about your own aunt in that way before you.

ALGERNON. My dear boy, I love hearing my relations abused. It is the only thing that makes me put up with them at all. Relations are simply a tedious pack of people, who haven't got the remotest knowledge of how to live, nor the smallest instinct about when to die.

JACK. Oh, that is nonsense!

ALGERNON. It isn't!

JACK. Well, I won't argue about the matter. You always want to argue about things.

ALGERNON. That is exactly what things were originally made for.

JACK. Upon my word, if I thought that, I'd shoot myself. . . . (*A pause.*) You don't think there is any chance of Gwendolen becoming like her mother in about a hundred and fifty years, do you, Algy?

ALGERNON. All women become like their mothers. That is their tragedy. No man does. That's his.

JACK. Is that clever?

ALGERNON. It is perfectly phrased! and quite as true as any observation in civilised life should be.

JACK. I am sick to death of cleverness. Everybody is clever nowadays. You can't go anywhere without meeting clever people. The thing has become an absolute public nuisance. I wish to goodness we had a few fools left.

ALGERNON. We have.

JACK. I should extremely like to meet them. What do they talk about?

ALGERNON. The fools? Oh! about the clever people, of course.

JACK. What fools!

ALGERNON. By the way, did you tell Gwendolen the truth about your being Ernest in town, and Jack in the country?

JACK (*in a very patronising manner*). My dear fellow, the truth isn't quite the sort of thing one tells to a nice, sweet, refined girl. What extraordinary ideas you have about the way to behave to a woman!

ALGERNON. The only way to behave to a woman is to make love to her, if she is pretty, and to some one else, if she is plain.

JACK. Oh, that is nonsense.

ALGERNON. What about your brother? What about the profligate Ernest?

JACK. Oh, before the end of the week I shall have got rid of him. I'll say he died in Paris of apoplexy. Lots of people die of apoplexy, quite suddenly, don't they?

ALGERNON. Yes, but it's hereditary, my dear fellow. It's a sort of thing that runs in families. You had much better say a severe chill.

JACK. You are sure a severe chill isn't hereditary, or anything of that kind?

ALGERNON. Of course it isn't!

JACK. Very well, then. My poor brother Ernest is carried off suddenly, in Paris, by a severe chill. That gets rid of him.

ALGERNON. But I though you said that . . . Miss Cardew was a little too much interested in your poor brother Ernest? Won't she feel his loss a good deal?

JACK. Oh, that is all right. Cecily is not a silly romantic girl, I am glad to say. She has got a capital appetite, goes long walks, and pays no attention at all to her lessons.

ALGERNON. I would rather like to see Cecily.

JACK. I will take very good care you never do. She is excessively pretty, and she is only just eighteen.

ALGERNON. Have you told Gwendolen yet that you have an excessively pretty ward who is only just eighteen?

JACK. Oh! one doesn't blurt these things out to people. Cecily and Gwendolen are perfectly certain to be extremely great friends. I'll bet you anything you like that half an hour after they have met, they will be calling each other sister.

ALGERNON. Women only do that when they have called each other a lot of other things first. Now, my dear boy, if we want to get a good table at Willis's, we really must go and dress. Do you know it is nearly seven?

JACK (irritably). Oh! it always is nearly seven.

ALGERNON. Well, I'm hungry.

JACK. I never knew you when you weren't. . . .

ALGERNON. What shall we do after dinner? Go to a theatre?

JACK. Oh no! I loathe listening.

ALGERNON. Well, let us go to the Club?

JACK. Oh, no! I hate talking.

ALGERNON. Well, we might trot round to the Empire at ten?

JACK. Oh, no! I can't bear looking at things. It is so silly.

ALGERNON. Well, what shall we do?

JACK. Nothing!

ALGERNON. It is awfully hard work doing nothing. However, I don't mind hard work where there is no definite object of any kind.

Enter LANE.

LANE. Miss Fairfax.

Enter GWENDOLEN.   LANE *goes out.*

ALGERNON. Gwendolen, upon my word!

GWENDOLEN. Algy, kindly turn your back. I have something very particular to say to Mr Worthing.

ALGERNON. Really, Gwendolen, I don't think I can allow this at all.

GWENDOLEN. Algy, you always adopt a strictly immoral attitude towards life. You are not quite old enough to do that. (ALGERNON *retires to the fireplace.*)

JACK. My own darling!

GWENDOLEN. Ernest, we may never be married. From the expression on mamma's face I fear we never shall. Few parents nowadays pay any regard to what their children say to them. The old-fashioned respect for the young is fast dying out. Whatever influence I ever had over mamma, I lost at the age of three. But although she may prevent us from becoming man and wife, and I may marry some one else, and marry often, nothing that she can possibly do can alter my eternal devotion to you.

JACK. Dear Gwendolen!

GWENDOLEN. The story of your romantic origin, as related to me by mamma, with unpleasing comments, has naturally stirred the deeper fibres of my nature. Your Christian name has an irresistible fascination. The simplicity of your character makes you exquisitely incomprehensible to me. Your town address at the Albany I have. What is your address in the country.

JACK. The Manor House, Woolton, Hertfordshire.

> ALGERNON, *who has been carefully listening, smiles to himself, and writes the address on his shirt-cuff. Then picks up the Railway Guide.*

GWENDOLEN. There is a good postal service, I suppose? It may be necessary to do something desperate. That of course will require serious consideration. I will communicate with you daily.

JACK. My own one!

GWENDOLEN. How long do you remain in town?

JACK. Till Monday.

GWENDOLEN. Good! Algy, you may turn round now.

ALGERNON. Thanks, I've turned round already.

GWENDOLEN. You may also ring the bell.

JACK. You will let me see you to your carriage, my own darling?

GWENDOLEN. Certainly.

JACK (*to* LANE, *who now enters*). I will see Miss Fairfax out.

LANE. Yes, sir. (JACK *and* GWENDOLEN *go off.*)

> LANE *presents several letters on a salver to* ALGERNON. *It is to be surmised that they are bills, as* ALGERNON, *after looking at the envelopes, tears them up.*

ALGERNON. A glass of sherry, Lane.

LANE. Yes, sir.

ALGERNON. To-morrow, Lane, I'm going Bunburying.

LANE. Yes, sir.

ALGERNON. I shall probably not be back till Monday. You can put up my dress clothes, my smoking jacket, and all the Bunbury suits . . .

LANE. Yes, sir. (*Handing sherry.*)

ALGERNON. I hope to-morrow will be a fine day, Lane.

LANE. It never is, sir.

ALGERNON. Lane, you're a perfect pessimist.

LANE. I do my best to give satisfaction, sir.

Enter JACK.   LANE *goes off.*

JACK. There's a sensible, intellectual girl! the only girl I ever cared for in my life. (ALGERNON *is laughing immoderately.*) What on earth are you so amused at?

ALGERNON. Oh, I'm a little anxious about poor Bunbury, that is all.

JACK. If you don't take care, your friend Bunbury will get you into a serious scrape some day.

ALGERNON. I love scrapes. They are the only things that are never serious.

JACK. Oh, that's nonsense, Algy. You never talk anything but nonsense.

ALGERNON. Nobody ever does.

JACK *looks indignantly at him, and leaves the room.*
ALGERNON *lights a cigarette, reads his shirt-cuff, and smiles.*

Act Drop

Second Act

SCENE

Garden at the Manor House. A flight of grey stone steps leads up to the house. The garden, an old-fashioned one, full of roses. Time of year, July. Basket chairs, and a table covered with books, are set under a large yew-tree.

MISS PRISM *discovered seated at the table.* CECILY *is at the the back watering flowers.*

MISS PRISM (*calling*). Cecily, Cecily! Surely such a utilitarian occupation as the watering of flowers is rather Moulton's duty than yours? Especially at a moment when intellectual pleasures await you. Your German grammar is on the table. Pray open it at page fifteen. We will repeat yesterday's lesson.

CECILY (*coming over very slowly*). But I don't like German. It isn't at all a becoming language. I know perfectly well that I look quite plain after my German lesson.

MISS PRISM. Child, you know how anxious your guardian is that you should improve yourself in every way. He laid particular stress on your German, as he was leaving for town yesterday. Indeed, he always lays stress on your German when he is leaving for town.

CECILY. Dear Uncle Jack is so very serious! Sometimes he is so serious that I think he cannot be quite well.

MISS PRISM (*drawing herself up*). Your guardian enjoys the best of health, and his gravity of demeanour is especially to be commended in one so comparatively young as he is. I know no one who has a higher sense of duty and responsibility.

CECILY. I suppose that is why he often looks a little bored when we three are together.

MISS PRISM. Cecily! I am surprised at you. Mr Worthing has many troubles in his life. Idle merriment and triviality would be out of place in his conversation. You must remember his constant anxiety about that unfortunate young man his brother.

CECILY. I wish Uncle Jack would allow that unfortunate young man, his brother, to come down here sometimes. We might have a good influence over him, Miss Prism. I am sure you certainly would. You know German, and geology, and things of that kind influence a man very much. (CECILY begins to write in her diary.)

MISS PRISM (shaking her head). I do not think that even I could produce any effect on a character that according to his own brother's admission is irretrievably weak and vacillating. Indeed I am not sure that I would desire to reclaim him. I am not in favour of this modern mania for turning bad people into good people at a moment's notice. As a man sows so let him reap. You must put away your diary, Cecily. I really don't see why you should keep a diary at all.

CECILY. I keep a diary in order to enter the wonderful secrets of my life. If I didn't write them down, I should probably forget all about them.

MISS PRISM. Memory, my dear Cecily, is the diary that we all carry about with us.

CECILY. Yes, but it usually chronicles the things that have never happened, and couldn't possibly have happened. I believe that Memory is responsible for nearly all the three-volume novels that Mudie sends us.

MISS PRISM. Do not speak slightingly of the three-volume novel, Cecily. I wrote one myself in earlier days.

CECILY. Did you really, Miss Prism? How wonderfully clever you are! I hope it did not end happily? I don't like novels that end happily. They depress me so much.

MISS PRISM. The good ended happily, and the bad unhappily. That is what Fiction means.

CECILY. I suppose so. But it seems very unfair. And was your novel ever published?

MISS PRISM. Alas! no. The manuscript unfortunately was abandoned. (CECILY *starts.*) I use the word in the sense of lost or mislaid. To your work, child, these speculations are profitless.

CECILY (*smiling*). But I see dear Dr Chasuble coming up through the garden.

MISS PRISM (*rising and advancing*). Dr Chasuble! This is indeed a pleasure.

    Enter CANON CHASUBLE.

CHASUBLE. And how are we this morning? Miss Prism, you are, I trust, well?

CECILY. Miss Prism has just been complaining of a slight headache. I think it would do her so much good to have a short stroll with you in the Park, Dr Chasuble.

MISS PRISM. Cecily, I have not mentioned anything about a headache.

CECILY. No, dear Miss Prism, I know that, but I felt instinctively that you had a headache. Indeed I was thinking about that, and not about my German lesson, when the Rector came in.

CHASUBLE. I hope, Cecily, you are not inattentive.

CECILY. Oh, I am afraid I am.

CHASUBLE. That is strange. Were I fortunate enough to be Miss Prism's pupil, I would hang upon her lips (MISS PRISM *glares.*) I spoke metaphorically. – My metaphor was drawn from bees. Ahem! Mr Worthing, I suppose, has not returned from town yet?

MISS PRISM. We do not expect him till Monday afternoon.

CHASUBLE. Ah yes, he usually likes to spend his Sunday in London. He is not one of those whose sole aim is enjoyment, as, by all accounts, that unfortunate young man his brother seems to be. But I must not disturb Egeria and her pupil any longer.

MISS PRISM. Egeria? My name is Laetitia, Doctor.

CHASUBLE (*bowing*). A classical allusion merely, drawn from the Pagan authors. I shall see you both no doubt at Evensong?

MISS PRISM. I think, dear Doctor, I will have a stroll with you. I find I have a headache after all, and a walk might do it good.

CHASUBLE. With pleasure, Miss Prism, with pleasure. We might go as far as the schools and back.

MISS PRISM. That would be delightful. Cecily, you will read your Political Economy in my absence. The chapter on the fall of the Rupee you may omit. It is somewhat too sensational. Even these metallic problems have their melodramatic side.

Goes down the garden with DR CHASUBLE.

CECILY (*picks up books and throws them back on table*). Horrid Political Economy! Horrid Geography! Horrid, horrid German!

Enter MERRIMAN *with a card on a salver.*

MERRIMAN. Mr Ernest Worthing has just driven over from the station. He has brought his luggage with him.

CECILY (*takes the card and reads it*). 'Mr Ernest Worthing, B. 4, The Albany, W.' Uncle Jack's brother! Did you tell him Mr Worthing was in town?

MERRIMAN. Yes, Miss. He seemed very much disappointed. I mentioned that you and Miss Prism were in the garden. He said he was anxious to speak to you privately for a moment.

CECILY. Ask Mr Ernest Worthing to come here. I suppose you had better talk to the housekeeper about a room for him.

MERRIMAN. Yes, Miss.

MERRIMAN *goes off*.

CECILY. I have never met any really wicked person before. I feel rather frightened. I am so afraid he will look just like every one else.

Enter ALGERNON, *very gay and debonair*.

He does!

ALGERNON (*raising his hat*). You are my little cousin Cecily, I'm sure.

CECILY. You are under some strange mistake. I am not little. In fact, I believe I am more than usually tall for my age. (ALGERNON *is rather taken aback*.) But I am your cousin Cecily. You, I see from your card, are Uncle Jack's brother, my cousin Ernest, my wicked cousin Ernest.

ALGERNON. Oh! I am not really wicked at all, cousin Cecily. You mustn't think that I am wicked.

CECILY. If you are not, then you have certainly been deceiving us all in a very inexcusable manner. I hope you have not been leading a double life, pretending to be wicked and being really good all the time. That would be hypocrisy.

ALGERNON (*looks at her in amazement*). Oh! Of course I have been rather reckless.

CECILY. I am glad to hear it.

ALGERNON. In fact, now you mention the subject, I have been very bad in my own small way.

CECILY. I don't think you should be so proud of that, though I am sure it must have been very pleasant.

ALGERNON. It is much pleasanter being here with you.

CECILY. I can't understand how you are here at all. Uncle Jack won't be back till Monday afternoon.

ALGERNON. That is a great disappointment. I am obliged to go up by the first train on Monday morning. I have a business appointment that I am anxious . . . to miss?

CECILY. Couldn't you miss it anywhere but in London?

ALGERNON. No: the appointment is in London.

CECILY. Well, I know, of course, how important it is not to keep a business engagement, if one wants to retain any sense of the beauty of life, but still I think you had better wait till Uncle Jack arrives. I know he wants to speak to you about your emigrating.

ALGERNON. About my what?

CECILY. Your emigrating. He has gone up to buy your outfit.

ALGERNON. I certainly wouldn't let Jack buy my outfit. He has no taste in neckties at all.

CECILY. I don't think you will require neckties. Uncle Jack is sending you to Australia.

ALGERNON. Australia! I'd sooner die.

CECILY. Well, he said at dinner on Wednesday night, that you would have to choose between this world, the next world, and Australia.

ALGERNON. Oh, well! The accounts I have received of Australia and the next world, are not particularly encouraging. This world is good enough for me, cousin Cecily.

CECILY. Yes, but are you good enough for it?

ALGERNON. I'm afraid I'm not that. That is why I want you to reform me. You might make that your mission, if you don't mind, cousin Cecily.

CECILY. I'm afraid I've no time, this afternoon.

ALGERNON. Well, would you mind my reforming myself this afternoon?

CECILY. It is rather Quixotic of you. But I think you should try.

ALGERNON. I will. I feel better already.

CECILY. You are looking a little worse.

ALGERNON. That is because I am hungry.

CECILY. How thoughtless of me. I should have remembered that when one is going to lead an entirely new life, one requires regular and wholesome meals. Won't you come in?

ALGERNON. Thank you. Might I have a buttonhole first? I never have any appetite unless I have a buttonhole first.

CECILY. A Maréchal Niel? (*Picks up scissors.*)

ALGERNON. No, I'd sooner have a pink rose.

CECILY. Why? (*Cuts a flower.*)

ALGERNON. Because you are like a pink rose, Cousin Cecily.

CECILY. I don't think it can be right for you to talk to me like that. Miss Prism never says such things to me.

ALGERNON. Then Miss Prism is a short-sighted old lady. (CECILY *puts the rose in his buttonhole.*) You are the prettiest girl I ever saw.

CECILY. Miss Prism says that all good looks are a snare.

ALGERNON. They are a snare that every sensible man would like to be caught in.

CECILY. Oh, I don't think I would care to catch a sensible man. I shouldn't know what to talk to him about.

They pass into the house. MISS PRISM *and* DR CHASUBLE *return.*

MISS PRISM. You are too much alone, dear Dr Chasuble. You should get married. A misanthrope I can understand – a womanthrope, never!

CHASUBLE (*with a scholar's shudder*). Believe me, I do not deserve so neologistic a phrase. The precept as well as the practice of the Primitive Church was distinctly against matrimony.

MISS PRISM (*sententiously*). That is obviously the reason why the Primitive Church has not lasted up to the present day. And you do not seem to realise, dear Doctor, that by persistently remaining single, a man converts himself into a permanent public temptation. Men should be more careful; this very celibacy leads weaker vessels astray.

CHASUBLE. But is a man not equally attractive when married?

MISS PRISM. No married man is ever attractive except to his wife.

CHASUBLE. And often, I've been told, not even to her.

MISS PRISM. That depends on the intellectual sympathies of the woman. Maturity can always be depended on. Ripeness can be trusted. Young women are green. (DR CHASUBLE *starts*). I spoke horticulturally. My metaphor was drawn from fruit. But where is Cecily?

CHASUBLE. Perhaps she followed us to the schools.

Enter JACK *slowly from the back of the garden. He is dressed in the deepest mourning, with crape hatband and black gloves.*

MISS PRISM. Mr Worthing!

CHASUBLE. Mr Worthing?

MISS PRISM. This is indeed a surprise. We did not look for you till Monday afternoon.

JACK (*shakes* MISS PRISM'S *hand in a tragic manner*). I have returned sooner than I expected. Dr Chasuble, I hope you are well?

CHASUBLE. Dear Mr Worthing, I trust this garb of woe does not betoken some terrible calamity?

JACK. My brother.

MISS PRISM. More shameful debts and extravagance?

CHASUBLE. Still leading his life of pleasure?

JACK (*shaking his head*). Dead!

CHASUBLE. Your brother Ernest dead?

JACK. Quite dead.

MISS PRISM. What a lesson for him! I trust he will profit by it.

CHASUBLE. Mr Worthing, I offer you my sincere condolence. You have at least the consolation of knowing that you were always the most generous and forgiving of brothers.

JACK. Poor Ernest! He had many faults, but it is a sad, sad blow.

CHASUBLE. Very sad indeed. Were you with him at the end?

JACK. No. He died abroad; in Paris, in fact. I had a telegram last night from the manager of the Grand Hotel.

CHASUBLE. Was the cause of death mentioned?

JACK. A severe chill, it seems.

MISS PRISM. As a man sows, so shall he reap.

CHASUBLE (*raising his hand*). Charity, dear Miss Prism, charity! None of us are perfect. I myself am peculiarly susceptible to draughts. Will the interment take place here?

JACK. No. He seems to have expressed a desire to be buried in Paris.

CHASUBLE. In Paris! (*Shakes his head.*) I fear that hardly points to any very serious state of mind at the last. You would no doubt wish me to make some slight allusion to this tragic domestic affliction next Sunday. (JACK *presses his hand convulsively.*) My sermon on the meaning of the manna in the wilderness can be adapted to almost any occasion, joyful, or, as in the present case, distressing. (*All sigh.*) I have preached it at harvest celebrations, christenings, confirmations, on days of humiliation and festal days. The last time I delivered it was in the Cathedral, as a charity sermon on behalf of the Society for the Prevention of Discontent among the Upper Orders. The Bishop, who was present, was much struck by some of the analogies I drew.

JACK. Ah! that reminds me, you mentioned christenings I think, Dr Chasuble? I suppose you know how to christen all right? (DR CHASUBLE *looks astounded.*) I mean, of course, you are continually christening, aren't you?

MISS PRISM. It is, I regret to say, one of the Rector's most constant duties in this parish. I have often spoken to the poorer classes on the subject. But they don't seen to know what thrift is.

CHASUBLE. But is there any particular infant in whom you are interested, Mr Worthing? Your brother was, I believe, unmarried, was he not?

JACK. Oh yes.

MISS PRISM (*bitterly*). People who live entirely for pleasure usually are.

JACK. But it is not for any child, dear Doctor. I am very fond of children. No! the fact is, I would like to be christened myself, this afternoon, if you have nothing better to do.

CHASUBLE. But surely, Mr Worthing, you have been christened already?

JACK. I don't remember anything about it.

CHASUBLE. But have you any grave doubts on the subject?

JACK. I certainly intend to have. Of course I don't know if the thing would bother you in any way, or if you think I am a little too old now.

CHASUBLE. Not at all. The sprinkling, and, indeed, the immersion of adults is a perfectly canonical practice.

JACK. Immersion!

CHASUBLE. You need have no apprehensions. Sprinkling is all that is necessary, or indeed I think advisable. Our weather is so changeable. At what hour would you wish the ceremony performed?

JACK. Oh, I might trot round about five if that would suit you.

CHASUBLE. Perfectly, perfectly! In fact I have two similar ceremonies to perform at that time. A case of twins that occurred recently in one of the outlying cottages on your own estate. Poor Jenkins the carter, a most hard-working man.

JACK. Oh! I don't see much fun in being christened along with other babies. It would be childish. Would half-past five do?

CHASUBLE. Admirably! Admirably! (*Takes out watch.*) And now, dear Mr Worthing, I will not intrude any longer into a house of sorrow. I would merely beg you not to be too much bowed down by grief. What seem to us bitter trials are often blessings in disguise.

MISS PRISM. This seems to me a blessing of an extremely obvious kind.

Enter CECILY *from the house.*

CECILY. Uncle Jack! Oh, I am pleased to see you back. But what horrid clothes you have got on! Do go and change them.

MISS PRISM. Cecily!

CHASUBLE. My child! my child! (CECILY *goes towards* JACK; *he kisses her brow in a melancholy manner.*)

CECILY. What is the matter, Uncle Jack? Do look happy! You look as if you had toothache, and I have got such a surprise for you. Who do you think is in the dining-room? Your brother!

JACK. Who?

CECILY. Your brother Ernest. He arrived about half an hour ago.

JACK. What nonsense! I haven't got a brother.

CECILY. Oh, don't say that. However badly he may have behaved to you in the past he is still your brother. You couldn't be so heartless as to disown him. I'll tell him to come out. And you will shake hands with him, won't you, Uncle Jack? (*Runs back into the house.*)

CHASUBLE. These are very joyful tidings.

MISS PRISM. After we had all been resigned to his loss, his sudden return seems to me peculiarly distressing.

JACK. My brother is in the dining-room? I don't know what it all means. I think it is perfectly absurd.

Enter ALGERNON *and* CECILY *hand in hand. They come slowly up to* JACK.

JACK. Good heavens! (*Motions* ALGERNON *away.*)

ALGERNON. Brother John, I have come down from town to tell you that I am very sorry for all the trouble I have given you, and that I intend to lead a better life in the future. (JACK *glares at him and does not take his hand.*)

CECILY. Uncle Jack, you are not going to refuse your own brother's hand?

JACK. Nothing will induce me to take his hand. I think his coming down here disgraceful. He knows perfectly well why.

CECILY. Uncle Jack, do be nice. There is some good in every one. Ernest has just been telling me about his poor invalid friend Mr Bunbury whom he goes to visit so often. And surely there must be much good in one who is kind to an invalid, and leaves the pleasures of London to sit by a bed of pain.

JACK. Oh! he has been talking about Bunbury, has he?

CECILY. Yes, he has told me all about poor Mr Bunbury, and his terrible state of health.

JACK. Bunbury! Well, I won't have him talk to you about Bunbury or about anything else. It is enough to drive one perfectly frantic.

ALGERNON. Of course I admit that the faults were all on my side. But I must say that I think that Brother John's coldness to me is peculiarly painful. I expected a more enthusiastic welcome, especially considering it is the first time I have come here.

CECILY. Uncle Jack, if you don't shake hands with Ernest I will never forgive you.

JACK. Never forgive me?

CECILY. Never, never, never!

JACK. Well, this is the last time I shall ever do it. (*Shakes hands with* ALGERNON *and glares.*)

CHASUBLE. It's pleasant, is it not, to see so perfect a reconciliation? I think we might leave the two brothers together.

MISS PRISM. Cecily, you will come with us.

CECILY. Certainly, Miss Prism. My little task of reconciliation is over.

CHASUBLE. You have done a beautiful action to-day, dear child.

MISS PRISM. We must not be premature in our judgments.

CECILY. I feel very happy. (*They all go off except* JACK *and* ALGERNON.)

JACK. You young scoundrel, Algy, you must get out of this place as soon as possible. I don't allow any Bunburying here.

Enter MERRIMAN.

MERRIMAN. I have put Mr Ernest's things in the room next to yours, sir. I suppose that is all right?

JACK. What?

MERRIMAN. Mr Ernest's luggage, sir. I have unpacked it and put it in the room next to your own.

JACK. His luggage?

MERRIMAN. Yes, sir. Three portmanteaus, a dressing-case, two hat-boxes, and a large luncheon-basket.

ALGERNON. I am afraid I can't stay more than a week this time.

JACK. Merriman, order the dog-cart at once. Mr Ernest has been suddenly called back to town.

MERRIMAN. Yes, sir. (*Goes back into the house.*)

ALGERNON. What a fearful liar you are, Jack. I have not been called back to town at all.

JACK. Yes, you have.

ALGERNON. I haven't heard any one call me.

JACK. Your duty as a gentleman calls you back.

ALGERNON. My duty as a gentleman has never interfered with my pleasures in the smallest degree.

JACK. I can quite understand that.

ALGERNON. Well, Cecily is a darling.

JACK. You are not to talk of Miss Cardew like that. I don't like it.

ALGERNON. Well, I don't like your clothes. You look perfectly ridiculous in them. Why on earth don't you go up and change? It is perfectly childish to be in deep mourning for a man who is actually staying for a whole week with you in your house as a guest. I call it grotesque.

JACK. You are certainly not staying with me for a whole week as a guest or anything else. You have got to leave . . . by the four-five train.

ALGERNON. I certainly won't leave you so long as you are in mourning. It would be most unfriendly. If I were in mourning you would stay with me, I suppose. I should think it very unkind if you didn't.

JACK. Well, will you go if I change my clothes?

ALGERNON. Yes, if you are not too long. I never saw anybody take so long to dress, and with such little result.

JACK. Well, at any rate, that is better than being always over-dressed as you are.

ALGERNON. If I am occasionally a little over-dressed, I make up for it by being always immensely over-educated.

JACK. Your vanity is ridiculous, your conduct an outrage, and your presence in my garden utterly absurd. However, you have got to catch the four-five, and I hope you will have a pleasant journey back to town. This Bunburying, as you call it, has not been a great success for you. (*Goes into the house.*)

ALGERNON. I think it has been a great success. I'm in love with Cecily, and that is everything.

Enter CECILY *at the back of the garden. She picks up the can and begins to water the flowers.*

But I must see her before I go, and make arrangements for another Bunbury. Ah, there she is.

CECILY. Oh, I merely came back to water the roses. I thought you were with Uncle Jack.

ALGERNON. He's gone to order the dog-cart for me.

CECILY. Oh, is he going to take you for a nice drive?

ALGERNON. He's going to send me away.

CECILY. Then have we got to part?

ALGERNON. I am afraid so. It's a very painful parting.

CECILY. It is always painful to part from people whom one has known for a very brief space of time. The absence of old friends one can endure with equanimity. But even a momentary separation from any one to whom one has just been introduced is almost unbearable.

ALGERNON. Thank you.

Enter MERRIMAN.

MERRIMAN. The dog-cart is at the door, sir. (ALGERNON *looks appealingly at* CECILY.)

CECILY. It can wait, Merriman . . . for . . . five minutes.

MERRIMAN. Yes, Miss.

Exit MERRIMAN.

ALGERNON. I hope, Cecily, I shall not offend you if I state quite frankly and openly that you seem to me to be in every way the visible personification of absolute perfection.

CECILY. I think your frankness does you great credit, Ernest. If you will allow me, I will copy your remarks into my diary. (*Goes over to table and begins writing in diary.*)

ALGERNON. Do you really keep a diary? I'd give anything to look at it. May I?

CECILY. Oh no. (*Puts her hand over it.*) You see, it is simply a very young girl's record of her own thoughts and impressions, and consequently meant for publication. When it appears in volume form I hope you will order a copy. But pray, Ernest, don't stop. I delight in taking down from dictation. I have reached 'absolute perfection.' You can go on. I am quite ready for more.

ALGERNON (*somewhat taken aback*). Ahem! Ahem!

CECILY. Oh, don't cough, Ernest. When one is dictating one should speak fluently and not cough. Besides, I don't know how to spell a cough. (*Writes as* ALGERNON *speaks.*)

ALGERNON (*speaking very rapidly*). Cecily, ever since I first looked upon your wonderful and incomparable beauty, I have dared to love you wildly, passionately, devotedly, hopelessly.

CECILY. I don't think that you should tell me that you love me wildly, passionately, devotedly, hopelessly. Hopelessly doesn't seem to make much sense, does it?

ALGERNON. Cecily!

Enter MERRIMAN.

MERRIMAN. The dog-cart is waiting, sir.

ALGERNON. Tell it to come round next week, at the same hour.

MERRIMAN (*looks at* CECILY, *who makes no sign*). Yes, sir.

MERRIMAN *retires.*

CECILY. Uucle Jack would be very much annoyed if he knew you were staying on till next week, at the same hour.

ALGERNON. Oh, I don't care about Jack. I don't care for anybody in the whole world but you. I love you, Cecily. You will marry me, won't you?

CECILY. You silly boy! Of course. Why, we have been engaged for the last three months.

ALGERNON. For the last three months?

CECILY. Yes, it will be exactly three months on Thursday.

ALGERNON. But how did we become engaged?

CECILY. Well, ever since dear Uncle Jack first confessed to us that he had a younger brother who was very wicked and bad, you of course have formed the chief topic of conversation between myself and Miss Prism. And of course a man who is much talked about is always very attractive. One feels there must be something in him, after all. I daresay it was foolish of me, but I fell in love with you, Ernest.

ALGERNON. Darling. And when was the engagement actually settled?

CECILY. On the 14th of February last. Worn out by your entire ignorance of my existence, I determined to end the matter one way or the other, and after a long struggle with myself I accepted you under this dear old tree here. The next day I bought this little ring in your name, and this is the little bangle with the true lover's knot I promised you always to wear.

ALGERNON. Did I give you this? It's very pretty, isn't it?

CECILY. Yes, you've wonderfully good taste, Ernest. It's the excuse I've always given for your leading such a bad life. And this is the box in which I keep all your dear letters. (*Kneels at table, opens box, and produces letters tied up with blue ribbon.*)

ALGERNON. My letters! But, my own sweet Cecily, I have never written you any letters.

CECILY. You need hardly remind me of that, Ernest. I remember only too well that I was forced to write your letters for you. I wrote always three times a week, and sometimes oftener.

ALGERNON. Oh, do let me read them, Cecily?

CECILY. Oh, I couldn't possibly. They would make you far too conceited. (*Replaces box.*) The three you wrote me after I had broken off the engagement are so beautiful, and so badly spelled, that even now I can hardly read them without crying a little.

ALGERNON. But was our engagement ever broken off?

CECILY. Of course it was. On the 22nd of last March. You can see the entry if you like. (*Shows diary.*) 'To-day I broke off my engagement with Ernest. I feel it is better to do so. The weather still continues charming.'

ALGERNON. But why on earth did you break it off? What had I done? I had done nothing at all. Cecily, I am very much hurt indeed to hear you broke it off. Particularly when the weather was so charming.

CECILY. It would hardly have been a really serious engagement if it hadn't been broken off at least once. But I forgave you before the week was out.

ALGERNON (*crossing to her, and kneeling*). What a perfect angel you are, Cecily.

CECILY. You dear romantic boy. (*He kisses her, she puts her fingers through his hair.*) I hope your hair curls naturally, does it?

ALGERNON. Yes, darling, with a little help from others.

CECILY. I am so glad.

ALGERNON. You'll never break off our engagement again Cecily?

CECILY. I don't think I could break it off now that I have actually met you. Besides, of course, there is the question of your name.

ALGERNON. Yes, of course. (*Nervously.*)

CECILY. You must not laugh at me, darling, but it had always been a girlish dream of mine to love some one whose name was Ernest. (ALGERNON *rises*, CECILY *also.*) There is something in that name that seems to inspire absolute confidence. I pity any poor married woman whose husband is not called Ernest.

ALGERNON. But, my dear child, do you mean to say you could not love me if I had some other name?

CECILY. But what name?

ALGERNON. Oh, any name you like – Algernon – for instance . . .

CECILY. But I don't like the name of Algernon.

ALGERNON. Well, my own dear, sweet, loving little darling, I really can't see why you should object to the name of Algernon. It is not at all a bad name. In fact, it is rather an aristocratic name. Half of the chaps who get into the Bankruptcy Court are called Algernon. But seriously, Cecily . . . (*Moving to her*) . . . if my name was Algy, couldn't you love me?

CECILY (*rising*). I might respect you, Ernest, I might admire your character, but I fear that I should not be able to give you my undivided attention.

ALGERNON. Ahem! Cecily! (*Picking up hat.*) Your Rector here is, I suppose, thoroughly experienced in the practice of all the rites and ceremonials of the Church?

CECILY. Oh, yes. Dr Chasuble is a most learned man. He

has never written a single book, so you can imagine how
much he knows.

ALGERNON. I must see him at once on a most important
christening – I mean on most important buinesss.

CECILY. Oh!

ALGERNON. I shan't be away more than half an hour.

CECILY. Considering that we have been engaged since February the 14th, and that I only met you to-day for the first time,
I think it is rather hard that you should leave me for so long
a period as half an hour. Couldn't you make it twenty
minutes?

ALGERNON. I'll be back in no time.

Kisses her and rushes down the garden.

CECILY. What an impetuous boy he is! I like his hair so much.
I must enter his proposal in my diary.

Enter MERRIMAN.

MERRIMAN. A Miss Fairfax has just called to see Mr Worthing. On very important business, Miss Fairfax states.

CECILY. Isn't Mr Worthing in his library?

MERRIMAN. Mr Worthing went over in the direction of the
Rectory some time ago.

CECILY. Pray ask the lady to come out here; Mr Worthing is
sure to be back soon. And you can bring tea.

MERRIMAN. Yes, Miss. (*Goes out.*)

CECILY. Miss Fairfax! I suppose one of the many good elderly
women who are associated with Uncle Jack in some of his
philanthropic work in London. I don't quite like women who
are interested in philanthropic work. I think it is so forward
of them.

Enter MERRIMAN.

MERRIMAN. Miss Fairfax.

Enter GWENDOLEN.

Exit MERRIMAN.

CECILY (*advancing to meet her*). Pray let me introduce myself to you. My name is Cecily Cardew.

GWENDOLEN. Cecily Cardew? (*Moving to her and shaking hands.*) What a very sweet name! Something tells me that we are going to be great friends. I like you already more than I can say. My first impressions of people are never wrong.

CECILY. How nice of you to like me so much after we have known each other such a comparatively short time. Pray sit down.

GWENDOLEN (*still standing up*). I may call you Cecily, may I not?

CECILY. With pleasure!

GWENDOLEN. And you will always call me Gwendolen won't you?

CECILY. If you wish.

GWENDOLEN. Than that is all quite settled, is it not?

CECILY. I hope so. (*A pause. They both sit down together.*)

GWENDOLEN. Perhaps this might be a favourable opportunity for my mentioning who I am. My father is Lord Bracknell. You have never heard of papa, I suppose?

CECILY. I don't think so.

GWENDOLEN. Outside the family circle, papa, I am glad to say, is entirely unknown. I think that is quite as it should be. The home seems to me to be the proper sphere for the man. And certainly once a man begins to neglect his domestic duties he becomes painfully effeminate, does he not? And I don't like that. It makes men so very attractive. Cecily, mamma, whose views on education are remarkably strict, has brought me up to be extremely short-sighted; it is part of her system; so do you mind my looking at you through my glasses?

CECILY. Oh! not at all, Gwendolen. I am very fond of being looked at.

GWENDOLEN (*after examining* CECILY *carefully through a lorgnette*). You are here on a short visit, I suppose.

CECILY. Oh no! I live here.

GWENDOLEN (*severely*). Really? Your mother, no doubt, or some female relative of advanced years, resides here also?

CECILY. Oh no! I have no mother, nor, in fact, any relations.

GWENDOLEN. Indeed?

CECILY. My dear guardian, with the assistance of Miss Prism, has the arduous task of looking after me.

GWENDOLEN. Your guardian?

CECILY. Yes, I am Mr Worthing's ward.

GWENDOLEN. Oh! It is strange he never mentioned to me that he had a ward. How secretive of him! He grows more interesting hourly. I am not sure, however, that the news inspires me with feelings of unmixed delight. (*Rising and going to her.*) I am very fond of you, Cecily; I have liked you ever since I met you! But I am bound to state that now that I know that you are Mr Worthing's ward, I cannot help expressing a wish you were – well, just a little older than you seem to be – and not quite so very alluring in appearance. In fact, if I may speak candidly —

CECILY. Pray do! I think that whenever one has anything unpleasant to say, one should always be quite candid.

GWENDOLEN. Well, to speak with perfect candour, Cecily, I wish that you were fully forty-two, and more than usually plain for your age. Ernest has a strong upright nature. He is the very soul of truth and honour. Disloyalty would be as impossible to him as deception. But even men of the noblest possible moral character are extremely susceptible to the influence of the physical charms of others. Modern, no less than Ancient History, supplies us with many most painful examples of what I refer to. If it were not so, indeed, History would be quite unreadable.

CECILY. I beg your pardon, Gwendolen, did you say Ernest?

GWENDOLEN. Yes.

CECILY. Oh, but it is not Mr Ernest Worthing who is my guardian. It is his brother – his elder brother.

GWENDOLEN (*sitting down again*). Ernest never mentioned to me that he had a brother.

CECILY. I am sorry to say they have not been on good terms for a long time.

GWENDOLEN. Ah! that accounts for it. And now that I think of it I have never heard any man mention his brother. The subject seems distasteful to most men. Cecily, you have lifted a load from my mind. I was growing almost anxious. It would have been terrible if any cloud had come across a friendship like ours, would it not? Of course you are quite, quite sure that it is not Mr Ernest Worthing who is your guardian?

CECILY. Quite sure. (*A pause.*) In fact, I am going to be his.

GWENDOLEN (*inquiringly.*) I beg your pardon?

CECILY (*rather shy and confidingly*). Dearest Gwendolen, there is no reason why I should make a secret of it to you. Our little country newspaper is sure to chronicle the fact next week. Mr Ernest Worthing and I are engaged to be married.

GWENDOLEN (*quite politely, rising*). My darling Cecily, I think there must be some slight error. Mr Ernest Worthing is engaged to me. The announcement will appear in the *Morning Post* on Saturday at the latest.

CECILY (*very politely, rising*). I am afraid you must be under some misconception. Ernest proposed to me exactly ten minutes ago. (*Shows diary.*)

GWENDOLEN (*examines diary through her lorgnette carefully*). It is certainly very curious, for he asked me to be his wife yesterday afternoon at 5.30. If you would care to verify the incident, pray do so. (*Produces diary of her own.*) I never travel without my diary. One should always have something sensational to read in the train. I am so sorry, dear Cecily, if it is any disappointment to you, but I am afraid I have the prior claim.

CECILY. It would distress me more than I can tell you, dear Gwendolen, if it caused you any mental or physical anguish, but I feel bound to point out that since Ernest proposed to you he clearly has changed his mind.

GWENDOLEN (*meditatively*). If the poor fellow has been entrapped into any foolish promise I shall consider it my duty to rescue him at once, and with a firm hand.

CECILY (*thoughtfully and sadly*). Whatever unfortunate entanglement my dear boy may have got into, I will never reproach him with it after we are married.

GWENDOLEN. Do you allude to me, Miss Cardew, as an entanglement? You are presumptuous. On an occaion of this kind it becomes more than a moral duty to speak one's mind. It becomes a pleasure.

CECILY. Do you suggest, Miss Fairfax, that I entrapped Ernest into an engagement? How dare you? This is no time for wearing the shallow mask of manner. When I see a spade I call it a spade.

GWENDOLEN (*satirically*). I am glad to say that I have never seen a spade. It is obvious that our social spheres have been widely different.

> *Enter* MERRIMAN, *followed by the footman. He carries a salver, table cloth, and plate stand.* CECILY *is about to retort. The presence of the servants exercises a restraining influence, under which both girls chafe.*

MERRIMAN. Shall I lay tea here as usual, Miss?

CECILY (*sternly, in a calm voice*). Yes, as usual. (MERRIMAN *begins to clear table and lay cloth. A long pause.* CECILY *and* GWENDOLEN *glare at each other.*)

GWENDOLEN. Are there many interesting walks in the vicinity, Miss Cardew?

CECILY. Oh! yes! a great many. From the top of one of the hills quite close one can see five counties.

GWENDOLEN. Five counties! I don't think I should like that; I hate crowds.

CECILY (*sweetly*). I suppose that is why you live in town? (GWENDOLEN *bites her lip, and beats her foot nervously with her parasol.*)

GWENDOLEN (*looking round*). Quite a well-kept garden this is, Miss Cardew.

CECILY. So glad you like it, Miss Fairfax.

GWENDOLEN. I had no idea there were any flowers in the country.

CECILY. Oh, flowers are as common here, Miss Fairfax, as people are in London.

GWENDOLEN. Personally I cannot understand how anybody manages to exist in the country, if anybody who is anybody does. The country always bores me to death.

CECILY. Ah! This is what the newspapers call agricultural depression, is it not? I believe the aristocracy are suffering very much from it just at present. It is almost an epidemic amongst them, I have been told. May I offer you some tea, Miss Fairfax?

GWENDOLEN (*with elaborate politeness*). Thank you. (*Aside.*) Detestable girl. But I require tea!

CECILY (*sweetly*). Sugar?

GWENDOLEN (*superciliously*). No, thank you. Sugar is not fashionable any more. (CECILY *looks angrily at her, takes up the tongs and puts four lumps of sugar into the cup.*)

CECILY (*severely*). Cake or bread and butter?

GWENDOLEN (*in a bored manner*). Bread and butter, please. Cake is rarely seen at the best houses nowadays.

CECILY (*cuts a very large slice of cake, and puts it on the tray*). Hand that to Miss Fairfax.

MERRIMAN *does so, and goes out with footman.* GWENDO-
LEN *drinks the tea and makes a grimace. Puts down cup
at once, reaches out her hand to the bread and butter, looks
at it, and finds it is cake. Rises in indignation.*

GWENDOLEN. You have filled my tea with lumps of sugar,
and though I asked most distinctly for bread and butter, you
have given me cake. I am known for the gentleness of my
disposition, and the extraordinary sweetness of my nature,
but I warn you, Miss Cardew, you may go too far.

CECILY (*rising*). To save my poor, innocent, trusting boy from
the machinations of any other girl there are no lengths to
which I would not go.

GWENDOLEN. From the moment I saw you I distrusted you.
I felt that you were false and deceitful. I am never deceived
in such matters. My first impressions of people are invariably
right.

CECILY. It seems to me, Miss Fairfax, that I am trespassing
on your valuable time. No doubt you have many other calls
of a similar character to make in the neighbourhood.

Enter JACK.

GWENDOLEN (*catching sight of him*). Ernest! My own Ernest!

JACK. Gwendolen! Darling! (*Offers to kiss her.*)

GWENDOLEN (*drawing back*). A moment! May I ask if you
are engaged to be married to this young lady? (*Points to*
CECILY.)

JACK (*laughing*). To dear little Cecily! Of course not! What
could have put such an idea into your pretty little head?

GWENDOLEN. Thank you. You may! (*Offers her cheek.*)

CECILY (*very sweetly*). I knew there must be some misunderstanding, Miss Fairfax. The gentleman whose arm is at
present round your waist is my guardian, Mr John Worthing.

GWENDOLEN. I beg your pardon?

CECILY. This is Uncle Jack.

GWENDOLEN (*receding*). Jack! Oh!

Enter ALGERNON.

CECILY. Here is Ernest.

ALGERNON (*goes straight over to* CECILY *without noticing any one else*). My own love! (*Offers to kiss her.*)

CECILY (*drawing back*). A moment, Ernest! May I ask you – are you engaged to be married to this young lady?

ALGERNON (*looking round*). To what young lady? Good heavens! Gwendolen!

CECILY. Yes! to good heavens, Gwendolen, I mean to Gwendolen.

ALGERNON (*laughing*). Of course not! What could have put such an idea into your pretty little head?

CECILY. Thank you. (*Presenting her cheek to be kissed.*) You may. (ALGERNON *kisses her.*)

GWENDOLEN. I felt there was some slight error, Miss Cardew. The gentleman who is now embracing you is my cousin, Mr. Algernon Moncrieff.

CECILY (*breaking away from* ALGERNON). Algernon Moncrieff! Oh! (*The two girls move towards each other and put their arms round each other's waists as if for protection.*)

CECILY. Are you called Algernon?

ALGERNON. I cannot deny it.

CECILY. Oh!

GWENDOLEN. Is your name really John?

JACK (*standing rather proudly*). I could deny it if I liked. I could deny anything if I liked. But my name certainly is John. It has been John for years.

CECILY (*to* GWENDOLEN). A gross deception has been practised on both of us.

GWENDOLEN. My poor wounded Cecily!

CECILY. My sweet wronged Gwendolen!

GWENDOLEN (*slowly and seriously*). You will call me sister, will you not? (*They embrace.* JACK *and* ALGERNON *groan and walk up and down.*)

CECILY (*rather brightly*). There is just one question I would like to be allowed to ask my guardian.

GWENDOLEN. An admirable idea! Mr Worthing, there is just one question I would like to be permitted to put to you. Where is your brother Ernest? We are both engaged to be married to your brother Ernest, so it is a matter of some importance to us to know where your brother Ernest is at present.

JACK (*slowly and hesitatingly*). Gwendolen – Cecily – it is very painful for me to be forced to speak the truth. It is the first time in my life that I have ever been reduced to such a painful position, and I am really quite inexperienced in doing anything of the kind. However, I will tell you quite frankly that I have no brother Ernest. I have no brother at all. I never had a brother in my life, and I certainly have not the smallest intention of ever having one in the future.

CECILY (*surprised*). No brother at all?

JACK (*cheerily*). None!

GWENDOLEN (*severely*). Had you never a brother of any kind?

JACK (*pleasantly*). Never. Not even of any kind.

GWENDOLEN. I am afraid it is quite clear, Cecily, that neither of us is engaged to be married to any one.

CECILY. It is not a very pleasant position for a young girl suddenly to find herself in. Is it?

GWENDOLEN. Let us go into the house. They will hardly venture to come after us there.

CECILY. No, men are so cowardly, aren't they?

They retire into the house with scornful looks.

JACK. This ghastly state of things is what you call Bunburying, I suppose?

ALGERNON. Yes, and a perfectly wonderful Bunbury it is. The most wonderful Bunbury I have ever had in my life.

JACK. Well, you've no right whatsoever to Bunbury here.

ALGERNON. That is absurd. One has a right to Bunbury anywhere one chooses. Every serious Bunburyist knows that.

JACK. Serious Bunburyist! Good heavens!

ALGERNON. Well, one must be serious about something, if one wants to have any amusement in life. I happen to be serious about Bunburying. What on earth you are serious about I haven't got the remotest idea. About everything, I should fancy. You have such an absolutely trivial nature.

JACK. Well, the only small satisfaction I have in the whole of this wretched business is that your friend Bunbury is quite exploded. You won't be able to run down to the country quite so often as you used to do, dear Algy. And a very good thing too.

ALGERNON. Your brother is a little off colour, isn't he, dear Jack? You won't be able to disappear to London quite so frequently as your wicked custom was. And not a bad thing either.

JACK. As for your conduct towards Miss Cardew, I must say that your taking in a sweet, simple, innocent girl like that is quite inexcusable. To say nothing of the fact that she is my ward.

ALGERNON. I can see no possible defence at all for your deceiving a brilliant, clever, thoroughly experienced young lady like Miss Fairfax. To say nothing of the fact that she is my cousin.

JACK. I wanted to be engaged to Gwendolen, that is all. I love her.

ALGERNON. Well, I simply wanted to be engaged to Cecily. I adore her.

JACK. There is certainly no chance of your marrying Miss Cardew.

ALGERNON. I don't think there is much likelihood, Jack, of you and Miss Fairfax being united.

JACK. Well, that is no business of yours.

ALGERNON. If it was my business, I wouldn't talk about it. (*Begins to eat muffins.*) It is very vulgar to talk about one's business. Only people like stockbrokers do that, and then merely at dinner parties.

JACK. How can you sit there, calmly eating muffins when we are in this horrible trouble, I can't make out. You seem to be perfectly heartless.

ALGERNON. Well, I can't eat muffins in an agitated manner. The butter would probably get on my cuffs. One should always eat muffins quite calmly. It is the only way to eat them.

JACK. I say it's perfectly heartless your eating muffins at all, under the circumstances.

ALGERNON. When I am in trouble, eating is the only thing that consoles me. Indeed, when I am in really great trouble, as any one who knows me intimately will tell you, I refuse everything except food and drink. At the present moment I am eating muffins because I am unhappy. Besides, I am particularly fond of muffins. (*Rising.*)

JACK (*rising*). Well, that is no reason why you should eat them all in that greedy way. (*Takes muffins from* ALGERNON.)

ALGERNON (*offering tea-cake*). I wish you would have tea-cake instead. I don't like tea-cake.

JACK. Good heavens! I suppose a man may eat his own muffins in his own garden.

ALGERNON. But you have just said it was perfectly heartless to eat muffins.

JACK. I said it was perfectly heartless of you, under the circumstances. That is a very different thing.

ALGERNON. That may be. But the muffins are the same. (*He seizes the muffin-dish from* JACK.)

JACK. Algy, I wish to goodness you would go.

ALGERNON. You can't possibly ask me to go without having some dinner. It's absurd. I never go without my dinner. No one ever does, except vegetarians and people like that.

Besides I have just made arrangements with Dr Chasuble to be christened at a quarter to six under the name of Ernest.

JACK. My dear fellow, the sooner you give up that nonsense the better. I made arrangements this morning with Dr Chasuble to be christened myself at 5.30, and I naturally will take the name of Ernest. Gwendolen would wish it. We can't both be christened Ernest. It's absurd. Besides, I have a perfect right to be christened if I like. There is no evidence at all that I have ever been christened by anybody. I should think it extremely probable I never was, and so does Dr Chasuble. It is entirely different in your case. You have been christened already.

ALGERNON. Yes, but I have not been christened for years.

JACK. Yes, but you have been christened. That is the important thing.

ALGERNON. Quite so. So I know my constitution can stand it. If you are not quite sure about your ever having been christened, I must say I think it rather dangerous your venturing on it now. It might make you very unwell. You can hardly have forgotten that some one very closely connected with you was very nearly carried off this week in Paris by a severe chill.

JACK. Yes, but you said yourself that a severe chill was not hereditary.

ALGERNON. It usen't to be, I know – but I daresay it is now. Science is always making wonderful improvements in things.

JACK (*picking up the muffin-dish*). Oh, that is nonsense; you are always talking nonsense.

ALGERNON. Jack, you are at the muffins again! I wish you wouldn't. There are only two left. (*Takes them.*) I told you I was particularly fond of muffins.

JACK. But I hate tea-cake.

ALGERNON. Why on earth then do you allow tea-cake to be served up for your guests? What ideas you have of hospitality!

JACK. Algernon! I have already told you to go. I don't want you here. Why don't you go!

ALGERNON. I haven't quite finished my tea yet! and there is still one muffin left. (JACK *groans, and sinks into a chair.* ALGERNON *still continues eating.*)

Act Drop

Third Act

SCENE

Morning-room at the Manor House.

GWENDOLEN *and* CECILY *are at the window, looking out into the garden.*

GWENDOLEN. The fact that they did not follow us at once into the house, as any one else would have done, seems to me to show that they have some sense of shame left.

CECILY. They have been eating muffins. That looks like repentance.

GWENDOLEN (*after a pause*). They don't seem to notice us at all. Couldn't you cough?

CECILY. But I haven't got a cough.

GWENDOLEN. They're looking at us. What effrontery!

CECILY. They approaching. That's very forward of them.

GWENDOLEN. Let us preserve a dignified silence.

CECILY. Certainly. It's the only thing to do now.

Enter JACK *followed by* ALGERNON. *They whistle some dreadful popular air from a British Opera.*

GWENDOLEN. This dignified silence seems to produce an unpleasant effect.

CECILY. A most distasteful one.

GWENDOLEN. But we will not be the first to speak

CECILY. Certainly not.

GWENDOLEN. Mr Worthing, I have something very particular to ask you. Much depends on your reply.

CECILY. Gwendolen, your common sense is invaluable. Mr Moncrieff, kindly answer me the following question. Why did you pretend to be my guardian's brother?

ALGERNON. In order that I might have an opportunity of meeting you.

CECILY (*to* GWENDOLEN). That certainly seems a satisfactory explanation, does it not?

GWENDOLEN. Yes, dear, if you can believe him.

CECILY. I don't. But that does not affect the wonderful beauty of his answer.

GWENDOLEN. True. In matters of grave importance, style, not sincerity is the vital thing. Mr Worthing, what explanation can you offer to me for pretending to have a brother? Was it in order that you might have an opportunity of coming up to town to see me as often as possible?

JACK. Can you doubt it, Miss Fairfax?

GWENDOLEN. I have the gravest doubts upon the subject. But I intend to crush them. This is not the moment for German scepticism. (*Moving to* CECILY.) Their explanations appear to be quite satisfactory, especially Mr Worthing's. That seems to me to have the stamp of truth upon it.

CECILY. I am more than content with what Mr Moncrieff said. His voice alone inspires one with absolute credulity.

GWENDOLEN. Then you think we should forgive them?

CECILY. Yes. I mean no.

GWENDOLEN. True! I had forgotten. There are principles at stake that one cannot surrender. Which of us should tell them? The task is not a pleasant one.

CECILY. Could we not both speak at the same time?

GWENDOLEN. An excellent idea! I nearly always speak at the same time as other people. Will you take the time from me?

CECILY. Certainly. (GWENDOLEN *beats time with uplifted finger.*)

GWENDOLEN and CECILY (*speaking together*). Your Christian names are still an insuperable barrier. That is all!

JACK and ALGERNON (*speaking together*). Our Christian names! Is that all? But we are going to be christened this afternoon.

GWENDOLEN (*to* JACK). For my sake you are prepared to do this terrible thing?

JACK. I am.

CECILY (*to* ALGERNON). To please me you are ready to face this fearful ordeal?

ALGERNON. I am!

GWENDOLEN. How absurd to talk of the equality of the sexes! Where questions of self-sacrifice are concerned, men are infinitely beyond us.

JACK. We are. (*Clasps hands with* ALGERNON.)

CECILY. They have moments of physical courage of which we women know absolutely nothing.

GWENDOLEN (*to* JACK). Darling!

ALGERNON (*to* CECILY). Darling! (*They fall into each other's arms.*)

> *Enter* MERRIMAN. *When he enters he coughs loudly, seeing the situation.*

MERRIMAN. Ahem! Ahem! Lady Bracknell!

JACK. Good heavens!

> *Enter* LADY BRACKNELL. *The couples separate in alarm.*
>
> *Exit* MERRIMAN.

LADY BRACKNELL. Gwendolen! What does this mean?

GWENDOLEN. Merely that I am engaged to be married to Mr Worthing, mamma.

LADY BRACKNELL. Come here. Sit down. Sit down immediately. Hesitation of any kind is a sign of mental decay in the young, of physical weakness in the old. (*Turns to* JACK.)

Apprised, sir, of my daughter's sudden flight by her trusty maid, whose confidence I purchased by means of a small coin, I followed her at once by a luggage train. Her unhappy father is, I am glad to say, under the impression that she is attending a more than usually lengthy lecture by the University Extension Scheme on the Influence of a permanent income on Thought. I do not propose to undeceive him. Indeed I have never undeceived him on any question. I would consider it wrong. But of course, you will clearly understand that all communication between yourself and my daughter must cease immediately from this moment. On this point, as indeed on all points, I am firm.

JACK. I am engaged to be married to Gwendolen, Lady Bracknell!

LADY BRACKNELL. You are nothing of the kind, sir. And now, as regards Algernon! . . . Algernon!

ALGERNON. Yes, Aunt Augusta.

LADY BRACKNELL. May I ask if it is in this house that your invalid friend Mr Bunbury resides?

ALGERNON (*stammering*). Oh! No! Bunbury doesn't live here. Bunbury is somewhere else at present. In fact, Bunbury is dead.

LADY BRACKNELL. Dead! When did Mr Bunbury die? His death must have been extremely sudden.

ALGERNON (*airily*). Oh! I killed Bunbury this afternoon. I mean poor Bunbury died this afternoon.

LADY BRACKNELL. What did he die of?

ALGERNON. Bunbury? Oh, he was quite exploded.

LADY BRACKNELL. Exploded! Was he the victim of a revolutionary outrage? I was not aware that Mr. Bunbury was interested in social legislation. If so, he is well punished for his morbidity.

ALGERNON. My dear Aunt Augusta, I mean he was found out! The doctors found out that Bunbury could not live, that is what I mean – so Bunbury died.

LADY BRACKNELL. He seems to have had great confidence in the opinion of his physicians. I am glad, however, that he made up his mind at the last to some definite course of action, and acted under proper medical advice. And now that we have finally got rid of this Mr Bunbury, may I ask, Mr Worthing, who is that young person whose hand my nephew Algernon is now holding in what seems to me a peculiarly unnecessary manner?

JACK. That lady is Miss Cecily Cardew, my ward. (LADY BRACKNELL *bows coldly to* CECILY.)

ALGERNON. I am engaged to be married to Cecily, Aunt Augusta.

LADY BRACKNELL. I beg your pardon?

CECILY. Mr Moncrieff and I are engaged to be married, Lady Bracknell.

LADY BRACKNELL (*with a shiver, crossing to the sofa and sitting down.*) I do not know whether there is anything peculiarly exciting in the air of this particular part of Hertfordshire, but the number of engagements that go on seems to me considerably above the proper average that statistics have laid down for our guidance. I think some preliminary inquiry on my part would not be out of place. Mr Worthing, is Miss Cardew at all connected with any of the larger railway stations in London? I merely desire information. Until yesterday I had no idea that there were any families or persons whose origin was a Terminus. (JACK *looks perfectly furious, but restrains himself.*)

JACK (*in a clear, cold voice*). Miss Cardew is the grand-daughter of the late Mr Thomas Cardew of 149 Belgrave Square, S.W.; Gervase Park, Dorking, Surrey; and the Sporran, Fifeshire, N.B.

LADY BRACKNELL. That sounds not unsatisfactory. Three addresses always inspire confidence, even in tradesmen. But what proof have I of their authenticity?

JACK. I have carefully preserved the Court Guides of the

period. They are open to your inspection, Lady Bracknell.

LADY BRACKNELL (*grimly*). I have known strange errors in that publication.

JACK. Miss Cardew's family solicitors are Messrs. Markby, Markby, and Markby.

LADY BRACKNELL. Markby, Markby, and Markby? A firm of the very highest position in their profession. Indeed I am told that one of the Mr Markby's is occasionally to be seen at dinner parties. So far I am satisfied.

JACK (*very irritably*). How extremely kind of you, Lady Bracknell! I have also in my possession, you will be pleased to hear, certificates of Miss Cardew's birth, baptism, whooping cough, registration, vaccination, confirmation, and the measles; both the German and the English variety.

LADY BRACKNELL. Ah! A life crowded with incident, I see; though perhaps somewhat too exciting for a young girl. I am not myself in favour of premature experiences! (*Rises, looks at her watch.*) Gwendolen! the time approaches for our departure. We have not a moment to lose. As a matter of form, Mr Worthing, I had better ask you if Miss Cardew has any little fortune?

JACK. Oh! about a hundred and thirty thousand pounds in the Funds. That is all. Good-bye, Lady Bracknell. So pleased to have seen you.

LADY BRACKNELL (*sitting down again*). A moment, Mr Worthing. A hundred and thirty thousand pounds! And in the Funds! Miss Cardew seems to me a most attractive young lady, now that I look at her. Few girls of the present day have any really solid qualities, any of the qualities that last, and improve with time. We live, I regret to say, in an age of surfaces. (*To* CECILY.) Come over here, dear. (CECILY *goes across.*) Pretty child! your dress is sadly simple, and your hair seems almost as Nature might have left it. But we can soon alter all that. A thoroughly experienced French maid produces a really marvellous result in a very brief space of time. I remember recommending one to young Lady Lancing, and after three months her own husband did not know her.

JACK. And after six months nobody knew her.

LADY BRACKNELL (*Glares at* JACK *for a few moments. Then bends, with a practised smile, to* CECILY.) Kindly turn round, sweet child. (CECILY *turns completely round.*) No, the side view is what I want. (CECILY *presents her profile.*) Yes, quite as I expected. There are distinct social possibilities in your profile. The two weak points in our age are its want of principle and its want of profile. The chin a little higher, dear. Style largely depends on the way the chin is worn. They are worn very high, just at present. Algernon!

ALGERNON. Yes, Aunt Augusta!

LADY BRACKNELL. There are distinct social possibilities in Miss Cardew's profile.

ALGERNON. Cecily is the sweetest, dearest, prettiest girl in the whole world. And I don't care twopence about social possibilities.

LADY BRACKNELL. Never speak disrespectfully of Society, Algernon. Only people who can't get into it do that. (*To* CECILY.) Dear child, of course you know that Algernon has nothing but his debts to depend upon. But I do not approve of mercenary marriages. When I married Lord Bracknell I had no fortune of any kind. But I never dreamed for a moment of allowing that to stand in my way. Well, I suppose I must give my consent.

ALGERNON. Thank you, Aunt Augusta.

LADY BRACKNELL. Cecily, you may kiss me!

CECILY (*kisses her*). Thank you, Lady Bracknell.

LADY BRACKNELL. You may also address me as Aunt Augusta for the future.

CECILY. Thank you, Aunt Augusta.

LADY BRACKNELL. The marriage, I think, had better take place quite soon.

ALGERNON. Thank you, Aunt Augusta.

CECILY. Thank you, Aunt Augusta.

LADY BRACKNELL. To speak frankly, I am not in favour of long engagements. They give people the opportunity of finding out each other's character before marriage, which I think is never advisable.

JACK. I beg pardon for interrupting you, Lady Bracknell, but this engagement is quite out of the question. I am Miss Cardew's guardian, and she cannot marry without my consent until she comes of age. That consent I absolutely decline to give.

LADY BRACKNELL. Upon what grounds may I ask? Algernon is an extremely, I may almost say an ostentatiously, eligible young man. He has nothing, but he looks everything. What more can one desire?

JACK. It pains me very much to have to speak frankly to you, Lady Bracknell, about your nephew, but the fact is that I do not approve at all of his moral character. I suspect him of being untruthful. (ALGERNON and CECILY look at him in indignant amazement.)

LADY BRACKNELL. Untruthful! My nephew Algernon? Impossible! He is an Oxonian.

JACK. I fear there can be no possible doubt about the matter. This afternoon during my temporary absence in London on an important question of romance, he obtained admission to my house by means of the false pretence of being my brother. Under an assumed name he drank, I've just been informed by my butler, an entire pint bottle of my Perrier-Jouet, Brut, '89; wine I was specially reserving for myself. Continuing his disgraceful deception, he succeeded in the course of the afternoon in alienating the affections of my only ward. He subsequently stayed to tea, and devoured every single muffin. And what makes his conduct all the more heartless is, that he was perfectly well aware from the first that I have no brother, that I never had a brother, and that I don't intend to have a brother, not even of any kind. I distinctly told him so myself yesterday afternoon.

LADY BRACKNELL. Ahem! Mr Worthing, after careful consideration I have decided entirely to overlook my nephew's conduct to you.

JACK. That is very generous of you, Lady Bracknell. My own decision, however, is unalterable. I decline to give my consent.

LADY BRACKNELL (to CECILY). Come here, sweet child. (CECILY goes over.) How old are you, dear?

CECILY. Well, I am really only eighteen, but I always admit to twenty when I go to evening parties.

LADY BRACKNELL. You are perfectly right in making some slight alteration. Indeed, no woman should ever be quite accurate about her age. It looks so calculating. . . . (In a meditative manner.) Eighteen, but admitting to twenty at evening parties. Well, it will not be very long before you are of age and free from the restraints of tutelage. So I don't think your guardian's consent is, after all, a matter of any importance.

JACK. Pray excuse me, Lady Bracknell, for interrupting you again, but it is only fair to tell you that according to the terms of her grandfather's will Miss Cardew does not come legally of age till she is thirty-five.

LADY BRACKNELL. That does not seem to me to be a grave objection. Thirty-five is a very attractive age. London society is full of women of the very highest birth who have, of their own free choice, remained thirty-five for years. Lady Dumbleton is an instance in point. To my own knowledge she has been thirty-five ever since she arrived at the age of forty, which was many years ago now. I see no reason why our dear Cecily should not be even still more attractive at the age you mention than she is at present. There will be a large accumulation of property.

CECILY. Algy, could you wait for me till I was thirty-five?

ALGERNON. Of course I could, Cecily. You know I could.

CECILY. Yes, I felt it instinctively, but I couldn't wait all that time. I hate waiting even five minutes for anybody. It always makes me rather cross. I am not punctual myself, I know, but I do like punctuality in others, and waiting, even to be married, is quite out of the question.

ALGERNON. Then what is to be done, Cecily?

CECILY. I don't know, Mr Moncrieff.

LADY BRACKNELL. My dear Mr Worthing, as Miss Cardew states positively that she cannot wait till she is thirty-five – a remark which I am bound to say seems to me to show a somewhat impatient nature – I would beg of you to reconsider your decision.

JACK. But my dear Lady Bracknell, the matter is entirely in your own hands. The moment you consent to my marriage with Gwendolen, I will most gladly allow your nephew to form an alliance with my ward.

LADY BRACKNELL (*rising and drawing herself up*). You must be quite aware that what you propose is out of the question.

JACK. Then a passionate celibacy is all that any of us can look forward to.

LADY BRACKNELL. That is the destiny I propose for Gwendolen. Algernon, of course, can choose for himself. (*Pulls out her watch.*) Come, dear, (GWENDOLEN *rises*) we have already missed five, if not six, trains. To miss any more might expose us to comment on the platform.

        Enter DR CHASUBLE.

CHASUBLE. Everything is quite ready for the christenings.

LADY BRACKNELL. The christenings, sir! Is not that somewhat premature?

CHASUBLE (*looking rather puzzled, and pointing to* JACK *and* ALGERNON). Both these gentlemen have expressed a desire for immediate baptism.

LADY BRACKNELL. At their age? The idea is grotesque and irreligious! Algernon, I forbid you to be baptized. I will not hear of such excesses. Lord Bracknell would be highly displeased if he learned that that was the way in which you wasted your time and money.

CHASUBLE. Am I to understand then that there are to be no christenings at all this afternoon?

JACK. I don't think that, as things are now, it would be of much practical value to either of us, Dr Chasuble.

CHASUBLE. I am grieved to hear such sentiments from you, Mr Worthing. They savour of the heretical views of the Anabaptists, views that I have completely refuted in four of my unpublished sermons. However, as your present mood seems to be one peculiarly secular, I will return to the church at once. Indeed, I have just been informed by the pewopener that for the last hour and a half Miss Prism has been waiting for me in the vestry.

LADY BRACKNELL (*starting*). Miss Prism! Did I hear you mention a Miss Prism?

CHASUBLE. Yes, Lady Bracknell. I am on my way to join her.

LADY BRACKNELL. Pray allow me to detain you for a moment. This matter may prove to be one of vital importance to Lord Bracknell and myself. Is this Miss Prism a female of repellent aspect, remotely connected with education?

CHASUBLE (*somewhat indignantly*). She is the most cultivated of ladies, and the very picture of respectability.

LADY BRACKNELL. It is obviously the same person. May I ask what position she holds in your household?

CHASUBLE (*severely*). I am a celibate, madam.

JACK (*interposing*). Miss Prism, Lady Bracknell, has been for the last three years Miss Cardew's esteemed governess and valued companion.

LADY BRACKNELL. In spite of what I hear of her, I must see her at once. Let her be sent for.

CHASUBLE (*looking off*). She approaches; she is nigh.

Enter MISS PRISM *hurriedly.*

MISS PRISM. I was told you expected me in the vestry, dear Canon. I have been waiting for you there for an hour and three-quarters. (*Catches sight of* LADY BRACKNELL, *who has fixed her with a stony glare.* MISS PRISM *grows pale and quails. She looks anxiously round as if desirous to escape.*)

LADY BRACKNELL (*in a severe, judicial voice*). Prism! (MISS PRISM *bows her head in shame.*) Come here, Prism! (MISS PRISM *approaches in a humble manner.*) Prism! Where is that baby? (*General consternation. The* CANON *starts back in horror.* ALGERNON *and* JACK *pretend to be anxious to shield* CECILY *and* GWENDOLEN *from hearing the details of a terrible public scandal.*) Twenty-eight years ago, Prism, you left Lord Bracknell's house, Number 104, Upper Grosvenor Street, in charge of a perambulator that contained a baby of the male sex. You never returned. A few weeks later, through the elaborate investigations of the Metropolitan police, the perambulator was discovered at midnight, standing by itself in a remote corner of Bayswater. It contained the manuscript of a three-volume novel of more than usually revolting sentimentality. (MISS PRISM *starts in involuntary indignation.*) But the baby was not there! (*Every one looks at* MISS PRISM.) Prism! Where is that baby? (*A pause.*)

MISS PRISM. Lady Bracknell, I admit with shame that I do not know. I only wish I did. The plain facts of the case are these. On the morning of the day you mention, a day that is for ever branded on my memory, I prepared as usual to take the baby out in its perambulator. I had also with me a somewhat old, but capacious hand-bag in which I had intended to place the manuscript of a work of fiction that I had written during my few unoccupied hours. In a moment of mental abstraction, for which I never can forgive myself, I deposited the manuscript in the bassinette, and placed the baby in the hand-bag.

JACK (*who has been listening attentively*). But where did you deposit the hand-bag?

MISS PRISM. Do not ask me, Mr Worthing.

JACK. Miss Prism, this a is matter of no small importance to me. I insist on knowing where you deposited the hand-bag that contained that infant.

MISS PRISM. I left it in the cloak-room of one of the larger railway stations in London.

JACK. What railway station?

MISS PRISM (*quite crushed*). Victoria. The Brighton line. (*Sinks into a chair.*)

JACK. I must retire to my room for a moment. Gwendolen, wait here for me.

GWENDOLEN. If you are not too long, I will wait here for you all my life.

Exit JACK *in great excitement.*

CHASUBLE. What do you think this means, Lady Bracknell?

LADY BRACKNELL. I dare not even suspect, Dr Chasuble. I need hardly tell you that in families of high position strange coincidences are not supposed to occur. They are hardly considered the thing.

Noises are heard overhead as if some one was throwing trunks about. Every one looks up.

CECILY. Uncle Jack seems strangely agitated.

CHASUBLE. Your guardian has a very emotional nature.

LADY BRACKNEL. This noise is extremely unpleasant. It sounds as if he was having an argument. I dislike arguments of any kind. They are always vulgar, and often convincing.

CHASUBLE (*looking up*). It has stopped now. (*The noise is redoubled.*)

LADY BRACKNELL. I wish he would arrive at some conclusion.

GWENDOLEN. This suspense is terrible. I hope it will last.

Enter JACK *with a hand-bag of black leather in his hand.*

JACK (*rushing over to* MISS PRISM.) Is this the hand-bag, Miss Prism? Examine it carefully before you speak. The happiness of more than one life depends on your answer.

MISS PRISM (*calmly*). It seems to be mine. Yes, here is the injury it received through the upsetting of a Gower Street omnibus in younger and happier days. Here is the stain on the lining caused by the explosion of a temperance beverage, an incident that occurred at Leamington. And here, on the lock, are my initials. I had forgotten that in an extravagant mood I had had them placed there. The bag is undoubtedly mine. I am delighted to have it so unexpectedly restored to me. It has been a great inconvenience being without it all these years.

JACK (*in a pathetic voice*). Miss Prism, more is restored to you than this hand-bag. I was the baby you placed in it.

MISS PRISM (*amazed*). You?

JACK (*embracing her*). Yes . . . mother!

MISS PRISM (*recoiling in indignant astonishment*). Mr Worthing! I am unmarried!

JACK. Unmarried! I do not deny that is a serious blow. But after all, who has the right to cast a stone against one who has suffered? Cannot repentance wipe out an act of folly? Why should there be one law for men, and another for women? Mother, I forgive you. (*Tries to embrace her again.*)

MISS PRISM (*still more indignant*). Mr Worthing, there is some error. (*Pointing to* LADY BRACKNELL.) There is the lady who can tell you who you really are.

JACK (*after a pause*). Lady Bracknell, I hate to seem inquisitive, but would you kindly inform me who I am?

LADY BRACKNELL. I am afraid that the news I have to give you will not altogether please you. You are the son of my poor sister, Mrs Moncrieff, and consequently Algernon's elder brother.

JACK. Algy's elder brother! Then I have a brother after all. I knew I had a brother! I always said I had a brother! Cecily, – how could you have ever doubted that I had a brother? (*Seizes hold of* ALGERNON.) Dr Chasuble, my unfortunate brother. Miss Prism, my unfortunate brother. Gwendolen, my unfortunate brother. Algy, you young scoundrel, you will have to treat me with more respect in the future. You have never behaved to me like a brother in all your life.

ALGERNON. Well, not till to-day, old boy, I admit. I did my best, however, though I was out of practice.

Shakes hands.

GWENDOLEN (*to* JACK.) My own! But what own are you? What is your Christian name, now that you have become some one else?

JACK. Good heavens! . . . I had quite forgotten that point. Your decision on the subject of my name is irrevocable, I suppose?

GWENDOLEN. I never change, except in my affections.

CECILY. What a noble nature you have, Gwendolen!

JACK. Then the question had better be cleared up at once. Aunt Augusta, a moment. At the time when Miss Prism left me in the hand-bag, had I been christened already?

LADY BRACKNELL. Every luxury that money could buy, including christening, had been lavished on you by your fond and doting parents.

JACK. Then I was christened! That is settled. Now, what name was I given? Let me know the worst.

LADY BRACKNELL. Being the eldest son you were naturally christened after your father.

JACK (*irritably*). Yes, but what was my father's Christian name?

LADY BRACKNELL (*meditatively*). I cannot at the present moment recall what the General's Christian name was. But I have no doubt he had one. He was eccentric, I admit. But only in later years. And that was the result of the Indian climate, and marriage, and indigestion, and other things of that kind.

JACK. Algy! Can't you recollect what our father's Christian name was?

ALGERNON. My dear boy, we were never even on speaking terms. He died before I was a year old.

JACK. His name would appear in the Army Lists of the period, I suppose, Aunt Augusta?

LADY BRACKNELL. The General was essentially a man of peace, except in his domestic life. But I have no doubt his name would appear in any military directory.

JACK. The Army Lists of the last forty years are here. These delightful records should have been my constant study. (*Rushes to bookcase and tears the books out.*) M. Generals . . . Mallam, Maxbohm, Magley, what ghastly names they have —Markby, Migsby, Mobbs, Moncrieff! Lieutenant 1840, Captain, Lieutenant-Colonel, Colonel, General 1869, Christian names, Ernest John. (*Puts book very quietly down and speaks quite calmly.*) I always told you, Gwendolen, my name was Ernest, didn't I? Well, it is Ernest after all. I mean it naturally is Ernest.

LADY BRACKNELL. Yes, I remember now that the General was called Ernest. I knew I had some particular reason for disliking the name.

GWENDOLEN. Ernest! My own Ernest! I felt from the first that you could have no other name!

JACK. Gwendolen, it is a terrible thing for a man to find out suddenly that all his life he has been speaking nothing but the truth. Can you forgive me?

GWENDOLEN. I can. For I feel that you are sure to change.

JACK. My own one!

CHASUBLE (*to* MISS PRISM). Laetitia! (*Embraces her.*)

MISS PRISM (*enthusiastically*). Frederick! At last!

ALGERNON. Cecily! (*Embraces her.*) At last!

JACK. Gwendolen! (*Embraces her.*) At last!

LADY BRACKNELL. My nephew, you seem to be displaying signs of triviality.

JACK. On the contrary, Aunt Augusta, I've now realised for the first time in my life the vital Importance of Being Earnest.

Tableau

Curtain

Notes

Act I

1 *Half-Moon Street* — a street in the fashionable and expensive West End of London.

1 *forte* — special talent — a slight play on words here, as the full name of the piano is the 'pianoforte'.

1 *your book* — a manservant in a wealthy household would keep a 'cellar book' recording all details about the stock of wine etc., its price and condition, and when and by whom it was drunk.

2 *lower orders* — the working classes, such as servants and industrial labourers.

3 *in town* — 'town' — at least in Southern England — always meant London.

3 *Why such reckless extravagance in one so young* — a question appropriate to a more dramatic situation than the discussion of cucumber sandwiches.

3 *propose to her* — ask her to marry him.

3-4 *Divorce Court was specially invented* — from 1858 a Divorce Court had the power to hear divorce cases, grant divorces and make orders about financial arrangements, custody of children, etc. Before 1858 a divorce had only been obtainable by a special Act of Parliament.

4 *Divorces are made in Heaven* — the actual saying is that *'marriages* are made in Heaven'.

4 *first cousin* — someone whose father or mother is brother or sister to one of one's own parents; a first cousin's children are one's *second* cousins.

4 *to clear up the whole question of Cecily* — to explain and resolve the situation concerning Cecily.

4 *Rings bell* — a bell in each room would be connected to the servants' quarters, to summon the servants.

4 *smoking-room* — large houses or apartments might include a

room where gentlemen withdrew to smoke, so that the smell (and
perhaps the conversation) would not annoy the ladies or sully the
rest of the house.

5   *Scotland Yard* — until 1890 the headquarters of the
Metropolitan Police Force. This name was and is still commonly
used to refer to the headquarters of the Metropolitan Police,
though in 1890 its headquarters moved from Scotland Yard to
New Scotland Yard nearby, and recently to new offices in Victoria.
'Scotland Yard' is also used colloquially to describe the Criminal
Investigation Department (C.I.D.) for London and the whole
country, which has its headquarters there.

5   *hard up* — short of money.

6   *Tunbridge Wells* — a quiet town in Southern England. Its
mineral water spring made it the resort of wealthy invalids.

6   *the Albany* — a block of exclusive and expensive London
apartments for single gentlemen, close to Piccadilly Circus.

7   *have the thing out* — 'to have it out with someone' is to
demand a full explanation of some misunderstanding or
disagreement.

7   *false impression . . . dentists always do* — 'to produce a false
impression' generally means to cause a misunderstanding. Dentists
would take a plaster impression of a patient's jaw in order to make
false teeth.

7   *guardian* — a child or young person's legal guardian is usually
his father or mother. An orphan can be placed legally under the
guardianship of some other person. Cecily is thus Jack's ward.

8   *the whole truth pure and simple* — a commonly used phrase,
emphasising the truthfulness of a statement.

8   *scrapes* — awkward situations or adventures, generally of a
childish kind.

8   *Willis's* — the celebrated and fashionable Almack's Assembly
Rooms (later called Willis's after the owner's niece who inherited
them) closed in 1890, then reopened as a restaurant.

9   *sent down* — when guests had assembled in the drawing room
(usually on the first floor) they went down to the dining room
(usually on the ground floor, nearer to the basement kitchens) in
pairs of one man and one woman, the most important pair going
first, an order that would be reflected in the seating round the
dinner table.

9   *place me next to* — a hostess arranged for her guests to sit in
a certain order round the dinner table, men and women alternating.

9 *washing one's clean linen in public* — the familiar expression would be 'to wash one's *dirty* linen in public' — that is, to make one's disreputable secrets common knowledge. Here, Algernon is objecting to an uninteresting *lack* of guilt.

9 *three is company and two is none* — the proverb is that '*two* is company and *three* is none', implying that lovers prefer not to be interrupted by others.

9 *the corrupt French Drama* — for the last fifty years . . . French plays of the period were popularly supposed to be concerned exclusively with adultery, e.g. the farces by such authors as Feydeau and Labiche.

10 *Wagnerian* — Since the characters in Wagner's operas are mostly large and powerful (requiring large and powerful singers, male and female) Lady Bracknell has obviously earned the description by ringing the bell loudly and with considerable force.

11 *ready money* — payment in cash, as opposed to credit. The upper class was accustomed to buying on account and not paying cash.

11 *crumpets* — yeast buns, served toasted and buttered, especially at tea time.

11 *quite gold from grief* — it was thought that grief could turn one's hair white. This merry widow has used hair-dye of a happier colour.

12 *put my table completely out* — (see note on 'place me next to', p. 9). The absence of one guest might spoil the hostess's seating plan, leaving an awkward number, or placing two enemies side by side.

12 *Exchange glances* — looking at one another briefly but significantly.

12 *shilly-shallying* — vacillation, constant changing of one's mind.

12 *arrange my music* — plan what music is to be played at a reception.

12 *reception* — a formal party for guests.

12 *the season* — the short period in early summer when balls, parties, and other entertainments were held in smart London society — mainly to arrange suitable marriages.

14 *domesticity* — shortened, familiar form.

14 *christened* — baptised; sprinkled with or immersed (see note on 'immersion' on p. 35) in water in a ceremony to give a 'Christian' (first) name, and to receive someone into the Church.

16 *engaged* — betrothed; promised to marry.

16 *will inform you* — the arrangement of marriages among upper

and middle class young people, commoner on the continent of
Europe, was never an invariable custom in England, as is clear in
literature from Shakespeare onwards, and was subject to the young
people's insubordination, as here. Lady Bracknell is clearly a firm
supporter of the system.

17 *tampers with natural ignorance.* — Ignorance is like a delicate
exotic fruit . . . this statement would conventionally be made about
innocence, not ignorance.

17 *Grosvenor Square* — fashionable square in the West End of
London, inhabited by the upper classes. 'Grosvenor' is pronounced
'Grow'v'ner'.

17 *In land* — an income 'in land' would be drawn from the rents
paid by tenant farmers on land owned by the person in question.

17 *the duties exacted from one after one's death* — death duties
(taxation of money and assets left in a will) had just been
introduced at the time the play was written, in 1894.

17 *It gives one position* — being the owner of land traditionally
gave the owner superior social status or position, but it was
becoming increasingly unreliable as a source of income.

17 *Belgrave Square* — fashionable square in the West End of
London.

18 *at six months' notice* — telling the tenant that he must leave
in six months.

18 *the unfashionable side* — although areas and even streets
could change abruptly in how 'fashionable' an address they were
considered, this distinction between two sides of the same
square is rather an exaggeration.

18 *Liberal Unionists . . . count as Tories* — a political party which
broke away from the Liberal Party over the latter's support for
Irish home rule. It became increasingly identified with the
Conservative Party, and so its members became almost respectable
in Lady Bracknell's view.

18 *come in the evening* — guests who were invited to come in
the evening after dinner were less important or intimate than those
invited to dine first with the family.

18 *Radical* — supporting the more socially progressive, reforming
views.

18 *purple of commerce* — purple, being a royal colour, suggests
a superior group among those who have made their money by trade
or industry, although the members of the inherited aristocracy
such as Lady Bracknell would normally despise any such
connection with commerce.

18 *rise from the ranks of the aristocracy* — 'rise from the ranks' is a metaphor taken from the army, where at that time only by exceptional merit could a private soldier in the lower ranks gain promotion. As the aristocracy considered itself the uppermost rank of society, Lady Bracknell is here speaking sarcastically.

19 *a handbag* — in the 1890's, a small suitcase to be carried by either sex.

19 *cloak-room* — in this context, a repository for luggage manned by an attendant.

19 *Victoria Station* — a large London railway station.

19 *the Brighton line* — on the platform serving the route to Brighton, a popular south-coast seaside resort.

20 *marry into a cloak-room* — inasmuch as the status or occupation of one's husband's family (e.g., trade, or the army) was imposed upon his wife, one was said to 'marry into trade' or 'marry into the army'. Lady Bracknell's phrase parodies this useage.

20 *Good morning!* — this is Lady Bracknell's way of being crushing and cutting to Jack. The time is in fact between 5.0 p.m. — tea-time (p.2) — and 'nearly seven' (p.22).

20 *Wedding March* — the music most commonly played when the bride enters the church at a wedding is 'The Wedding March' from Mendelssohn's incidental music to Shakespeare's *A Midsummer Night's Dream*.

20 *right as a trivet* — all right, causing no problems. A trivet was an iron stand for a pot or kettle.

20 *Gorgon* — Greek mythological creature that turned people to stone with its gaze.

21 *make love to* — in the 1890's, *talk* about love to.

22 *feel his loss* — be upset by his death.

22 *capital* — very good, hearty.

22 *ward* — note on 'guardian', p.7.

22 *called each other a lot of other things first* — insulted and called each other unpleasant names.

22 *go and dress* — change into evening clothes — formal dress worn for dinner and in the evening.

23 *the Club* — gentlemen's clubs in London (many of which still exist) were used as meeting places by members.

23 *the Empire* — music hall in Leicester Square, famous for its 'promenade', which had been attacked only the year before (1894) as a haunt of vice by a Mrs Chant in her Purity Campaign. A highly topical reference.

23 *the old-fashioned respect for the young* — the usual phrase would be 'respect for the old', which was urged upon disrespectful young people.

24 *Hertfordshire* — County just north of London; much more accessible than Shropshire.

24 *ring the bell* — (see note on p.4).

25 *scrape* — (see note on p.8).

Act 2

26 *Basket chairs* — chairs made of wickerwork, usually intertwined willow twigs.

27 *becoming* — something which 'becomes' one enhances one's appearance or personality.

27 *As a man sows, so shall he reap* — proverb adapted from the Bible; 'Whatsoever a man soweth that shall he also reap' (Galatians 6,7).

27 *Mudie* — Mudie's Library was an old-established lending library which also exchanged books by post.

28 *Fiction* — there is the hint of a pun here between fiction as imaginative literature and fiction as opposed to truth, i.e. as untruth.

28 *abandoned* Miss Prism means 'lost or mislaid', but Cecily understands 'abandoned' in the sense of 'morally lost and depraved'.

28 *Canon* — A clergyman attached to a cathedral. In this case, Canon Cashuble is the clergyman in charge of the local parish also. (Cf. *Rector* below).

28 *Rector* — A clergyman of the Church of England performing the duties connected with the church (religious services, etc.,) for a particular parish (distinguished from 'vicar', since his income was formerly dependent upon tithes).

28 *hang upon her lips* — listen to every word with fascinated attention.

28 *My metaphor was drawn from bees* — Since bees hang upon flowers with busy concentration.

29 *Egeria* — in Roman mythology, one of the Muses; proverbially used of a woman who inspires someone.

29 *Evensong* — the usual evening religious service.

29 *Political Economy* — here used for the study of economics generally. At this period it would be considered rather an 'unsuitable' subject for a young lady.

29 *Rupee* — a unit of currency in India, which was at this period part of the British Empire.

31 *Australia* — at one time criminals were transported to
Australia as a punishment; by this period Australia (being almost
as far away from England as possible) was considered a good place
to send unsatisfactory members of respectable families, for a
second chance to succeed, or to be forgotten.

31 *this world, the next world* — life and death.

31 *Quixotic* — reference to the impractical hero of Cervantes'
Don Quixote, implying idealism and unprofitable self-sacrifice.

32 *Maréchal Niel* — a variety of rose.

32 *womanthrope . . . neologistic* — Miss Prism is making up this
word to mean woman hater, on the analogy of misanthrope. The
correct word would be 'misogynist'. In coining her new word or
'neologism', Miss Prism was being 'neologistic'.

32 *weaker vessels* — Miss Prism means 'women' generally, though
according to the Bible 'weaker vessel' refers to a wife (1 Peter 3,7).

33 *deepest mourning, with crape hatband* — it was customary to
wear mourning — that is, black clothes — after the death of a
relative or friend; convention dictated the deepest (most complete)
mourning for closest relatives. Black crape was particularly
popular for mourning during the Victorian period.

34 *As a man sows* — (see note on p.27).

34 *Paris* — Paris was popularly considered a city of sin and
frivolity (cf. note on 'the corrupt French drama', p.9).

34 *the manna in the wilderness* — this refers to the miraculous
supply of food to the Israelites in the wilderness (Exodus, 16),
and is not at all appropriate to the death of an acquaintance.

34 *Society for the Prevention of Discontent among the Upper
Orders* — it was of course the 'Lower Orders' whose discontent it
was thought desirable to prevent.

34 *I regret to say* — Miss Prism is regretting the high rate of
births in the neighbourhood.

35 *the immersion of adults* — Christening (baptism) in the Church
of England is generally accomplished by a token sprinkling of
water, but certain sects, e.g. the Baptists, require total immersion.

35 *canonical* — according to the rules or 'canons' of the Church.

35 *trot round* — come round (slang of the period).

35 *a case of twins* — 'a case of' usually introduces the name of
an illness or disease.

35 *blessings in disguise* — conventional words of comfort:
misfortune may turn out to have been for the best.

38 *port manteaus* — large travelling cases. The amount of
luggage is excessive, especially for a stay of only a week.

38 *dog-cart* — a light, horse-drawn, two-wheeled vehicle.

38 *four-five* — five minutes past four o'clock.

40 *Ahem* — this is how a throat-clearing cough is conventionally spelt.

40 *Hopelessly* — Cecily might be expected to object modestly to the extravagance of 'wildly' and 'passionately', but in fact is only concerned to suggest that Algernon's love is *not* hopeless.

41 *engaged* — engaged to be married.

41 *14th of February* — St. Valentine's Day, when traditionally birds chose their mates and lovers their partners.

43 *Bankruptcy Court* — Court where the affairs of a would-be bankrupt were discussed. Algernon implies that this is much frequented by the aristocracy.

43-44 *He had never written a single book* — Cecily is implying how foolish most 'serious' books are.

44 *in no time* — almost at once.

44 *forward* — brazen, immodest — usually the application is to a 'forward' woman.

45 *The home seems to me the proper sphere for the man* — this statement is, of course, usually made about 'the woman'.

47 *The announcement will appear in the Morning Post* — most newspapers contained columns in which the upper and middle classes could pay to insert announcements of engagements, marriages, births, and deaths in their family. The *Morning Post* was a 'respectable', very Conservative daily newspaper.

48 *When I see a spade I call it a spade* — to 'call a spade a spade' is a well-known saying implying complete frankness, without hypocrisy or even politeness.

49 *anybody who is anybody* — anybody who is important, socially significant.

49 *agricultural depression* — literally, a decline in the prosperity of farming (not, as Cecily implies, boredom suffered through living in the country).

53 *exploded* — found out. The deception is revealed.

53 *off colour* — slightly unwell.

54 *business* — there is a punning contrast here between Jack's meaning ('anything that concerns you') and Algernon's narrower meaning of 'financial affairs' — about which it was not considered good manners to talk.

54 *go without my dinner* — to 'go without' dinner is not to have dinner at all. Jack only wishes Algernon to go away without having dinner at his house.

55 *constitution* — state of health.
55 *carried off* — killed (usually, as here, by an illness).

Act 3

57 *forward* — (see note on p.44).
57 *dreadful popular air* — (see Commentary for Wilde's connections with Gilbert and Sullivan opera).
58 *German scepticism* — German scholarship in theology and philosophy had gained a reputation for destructive scepticism.
58 *stamp of truth* — convincing appearance of truth.
59 *talk of the equality of the sexes* — a current issue, with much talk of 'the New Woman', such as Nora in Ibsen's *A Doll's House* and Vivie in Bernard Shaw's *Mrs Warren's Profession,* written in 1893. Gwendolen and Cecily, however, show few other signs of feminist awareness.
60 *University Extension Scheme* — scheme for providing educational lectures and classes for the general public. The Universities of Oxford, Cambridge, and London each had such an organisation.
60 *exploded* — (see note p.53).
61 *laid down for our guidance* — statistics, of course, should reflect phenomena that already exist, and not guide people's behaviour.
61 *Dorking, Surrey* — country town near enough to London to make its neighbourhood convenient — and expensive — as the site of a country house.
61 *Fifeshire, N.B.* — N.B. stands for North Britain — that is, Scotland. Rich persons might own a house in Scotland so that they could pursue the country 'sports' of hunting, shooting (notably grouse), and fishing.
61 *Court Guides* — Debrett's and other (generally annual) publications recording 'who was who' at court and in the aristocracy.
62 *seen at dinner parties* — this shows that Mr Markby is socially acceptable to those who give upper-class dinner parties, and is thus superior to most members of his profession who are not so acceptable.
62 *the Funds* — stock issued by the Government, considered a very safe investment.
63 *her own husband did not know her* — 'her own husband (or mother, etc.) did not know her' is a phrase often used to describe

the effects of a great change in someone's appearance.

63 *nobody knew her* – here means 'nobody would accept her socially'. The implication is that Lady Lancing's new, elegant appearance has led her into socially unacceptable, possibly immoral behaviour.

63 *But I never dreamed for a moment of allowing that to stand in my way* – this would normally be used in the opposite sense, of a rich person unselfishly ignoring the beloved's poverty.

64 *comes of age* – legally attains full adult status. At this period, this was usually at the age of twenty-one, though for specific purposes other ages could be stipulated; for instance, 'Miss Cardew does not come legally of age till she is thirty-five' (p.65).

64 *Oxonian* – graduate of Oxford University. Does not, of course, necessarily have any bearing on Algernon's truthfulness.

64 *Perrier-Jouet, Brut, '89* – superior champagne, of the vintage of 1889.

66 *out of the question* – impossible.

66 *expose us to comment* – make people talk about us.

67 *Anabaptists* – a sixteenth-century Christian sect which preached a new social organisation with absolute equality and community of goods – and also was opposed to infant baptism.

68 *Upper Grosvenor Street* – street in the fashionable and expensive West End of London, off Grosvenor Square (see note on p.17).

68 *Bayswater* – an area of West London, not at all fashionable in the 1890's.

68 *bassinette* – a type of perambulator.

69 *considered the thing* – considered the conventional and proper behaviour.

70 *Gower Street omnibus* – Gower Street is just north of London's West End. An omnibus would at this period be horse-drawn, and the upper-class would not travel in it.

70 *temperance beverage, an incident that occurred at Leamington* – 'temperance' implies total abstinence from alcohol: thus a temperance beverage was any drink said not to contain alcohol. Leamington was a spa much visited for the sake of its mineral waters.

72 *Army Lists* – a monthly distribution list included officers on active service. The quarterly list gave the seniority, appointments, and war services of officers in detail.